I0814432

Cuisines of Odesa

RECIPES AND STORIES
FROM UKRAINE'S HISTORIC CITY

MARIA KALENSKA

weldonowen

MDCCCLXXXVII
LXVII RESTITUTUM

CONTENTS

Foreword by Felicity Spector

The first time I visited Odesa, as the summer of 2022 was fading into autumn, I was on my own: Maria had planned to meet me as soon as I arrived, but she had been delayed at the border and wouldn't get there until the following day. She sent me a list of places I could explore, but the first one was cordoned off, and at the next, I got told off by a soldier for stupidly taking out my phone to translate a sign that screamed "under no circumstances take any photos," and then the air-raid siren came on when I was in the middle of the park. I could see the Black Sea shimmering somewhere in the distance as I waited under the distinctly inadequate shelter of some trees, and I thought that I would never be able to connect with Odesa at all. Then Maria arrived, and I saw the city through her eyes, and everything changed.

She swept me along to one of the food markets, on the edge of the city near her old apartment. It was a truly magical sight, rows of beautiful produce arranged so neatly that every apple seemed to have been polished by hand. Huge pumpkins were stacked into towers. Some stalls were covered by thickets of fresh dill and parsley, bunches of spring onions, and jars of beans and nuts. There was an entire room devoted to dairy, cottage cheese of all kinds, and sour cream so thick and rich that it was yellow like butter. Maria knew exactly which stalls to visit, holding out the back of her hand for a dollop of cream to try, passing me slices of salty brynza and the caramel-colored curd cheese made from baked milk that is special to Odesa. We picked up eggs displayed in a mysterious sorting system that I could not comprehend at all, but Maria shopped like an absolute expert. Back at her flat she whipped up a batch of my favorite syrniki pancakes, and we ate smoky dried prunes stuffed with walnuts and slices of fermented apple. We took a taxi down to the beach and Maria's favorite hotel, which had the most incredible view of the sea. Maria managed to rustle up some cups of coffee from the deserted cafe, and as we watched the waves gently lapping the shore, she had kindled a love affair with Odesa that I would never forget.

Walking the streets with Maria was an education in itself. There seemed to be nothing she did not know about the city, from its rich cultural history to its architecture and food. "Everything in Odesa is just one phone call away," she told me once, after spending around three minutes finding someone I thought would be impossible to track down. She was passionate about her favorite region of Bessarabia, and often implored me to buy a house in the prettiest village there. She took me there on several trips, and I learned the true meaning of hospitality every time we were invited into someone's home for "just a cup of tea." Inevitably they would cover an entire table with many dishes of food, and you couldn't leave your plate empty for a moment. There were magical evenings sharing slices of sweet bread swirled with poppy seeds baked by a retired teacher, watching the sun go down over Lake Yalpuh as a flock of birds took off over the horizon. She took me around restaurants in Odesa, where I discovered the joys of local dishes like forshmak, a version of Jewish chopped herring, and my beloved syrniki pancakes made with baked milk curd cheese. I couldn't think of a better person to write about the magic of Odesa's food and the incredible diversity that makes it so unique.

I began inviting myself along to her book shoots when she visited people in the city who had a treasured family recipe, deeply rooted in some part of Odesan culture. Everything was meticulously planned, from picking out the best-looking ingredients at the market to every aspect of the cooking process. She had such a strong vision of what she wanted, and directed her shoots with complete confidence, cajoling her subjects into narrow shards of light. We would arrive by taxi with bunches of flowers and baskets of fruit at various apartments, where Sasha, the young photographer, balanced precariously on chairs and

stood on tiptoe, camera aloft, capturing the perfect shot. And, of course, the best part was trying the dishes when the photographs were done. The intricate stuffed chicken made by Maria's mother-in-law, who had the contents of an entire prep kitchen stored neatly in her fridge. The apple vertuta made by our friend Kostya's mother, her hands stretching the impossibly thin dough so expertly that she barely needed to look down. There were nut- and prune-filled pastries, baked in a shallow bath of sunflower oil, a local Jewish lady's recipe, that were crunchy and crumbly and impossible to stop at one slice. And a baked cheesecake studded with golden raisins made by a young woman in an impeccably stylish flat and an outfit to match, six-inch heels and an apron embroidered with lace.

But Maria's project was about far more than recipes: It will become an important historical document too. Odesa has endured so much during these long years of war. Most nights have been punctuated by the howl of air-raid sirens and the sound of explosions in the sky and down at the port. Walking around town, it is impossible to escape the scars of war, the monuments masked by sandbags, and the buildings disfigured by Russian missiles or drones. There were days when there was no electricity, and times when we had to suddenly abandon photo shoots because ballistic missiles were on the way, and we had to rush downstairs to the basement. After the Russians blew up the Kakhovka dam in 2023, debris washed up hundreds of miles away on Odesa's beaches: The Black Sea was murky with flotsam, and the toxins in the water meant it was impossible to buy fresh fish. But Maria never gave up, even if many of her plans had to be endlessly rescheduled. Together with her longtime friend and photographer colleague Oleksander, they covered the back wall of our Bake for Ukraine office in photographs: each beautiful image of food echoed by a view of the city. The wall of photographs was itself a work of art: a living, breathing monument to this magnificent place and its centuries of history, at a time when Russia was steadily trying to destroy it, piece by piece.

Maria did not want her book to be about war, but about love: for her city, and for its food. And to witness so many of those dishes being made was an absolute privilege. This is how Odesa carries on, despite the missiles and the displaced people and the horrific losses that mount day by day. To read Maria's book, and to make her recipes, will be like having a personal invitation into this world, and a beautiful, complex, multicultural city that is full of love and life.

DOMUS SOLIS

Introduction

Nothing happens in Odesa without food. It is how we celebrate love and life and generosity—it is born from our history, our culture, and our diversity.

And if food is in our blood, the sea is in our soul. If I feel stressed, happy, or sad, I walk down to the sea, where the sound of the waves and the taste of salt in the air give me both energy and calm.

Everything in Odesa takes place around the table. We meet new members of the family, say farewell to those who pass away, do business, sort out relationships, have debates, discuss rising prices, get married, get divorced. Food is far more than simple nourishment: It is the way we champion our differences and our similarities; it is our past and our future.

This book was conceived as a gift to Odesa. I was born and grew up here, and like most Odesans, I am a fusion of different ethnicities: My background is a mix of Ukrainian and Greek. The idea to write the book came to me in 2014 when I moved from my hometown to London and suddenly saw the uniqueness of my city through the eyes of an outsider. I realized that the multicultural diversity of Odesan food is like a patchwork quilt, each element adding to the whole and creating something truly unique. I had been working on the book when, in 2022, the war gave me a new impetus. So, I found a hundred Odesan families, most of them based in Odesa along with some who have moved to twelve other cities, and collected their recipes and their stories—sometimes difficult, sometimes happy, often both at the same time. I wanted to tell the world what was so special about Odesa and why everyone should visit it. Anyone who's been here at least once will forever carry a small part of the city in their heart, along with the hope of returning to the shores of the bluest Black Sea in the world. *Laskavo prosimo.* Welcome.

OUR HISTORY

Odesa has always been one of Ukraine's most beautiful and important cities, thanks to its rich history, eclectic architecture, and cultural heritage. In 2022, Odesa was granted UNESCO's protected status. Situated in the south of Ukraine, the city is blessed with a lot of sunshine. Nestled between the wild steppes and the balmy Black Sea, Odesa has the vibrant region of Bessarabia looming over it, an area covered in vineyards, pastures, farms, and little villages full of wild roses, where people still bake bread in the shape of the sun. This is the place of myths, wine, and freedom—cosmopolitan, noisy, welcoming, and maddening, all at the same time.

Over the centuries Odesa and the surrounding area have been populated by Greeks, Italians, Ukrainians, Jews, and Germans, among others, since this has always been a vital port city and therefore a critical trading center. The eminent British photographer Ian Berry, who took lots of images of Odesa in the 1980s, dubbed the city The Marseille of Ukraine. Like its French counterpart, Odesa is a melting pot of people from around the world, a place of high energy, lots of sunshine, and the sea. People have been coming here to escape poverty, famine, lack of work, wars, and even genocides. They've been arriving with empty pockets and often broken hearts, determined to start all over again: to work, to learn, and to enjoy life, no matter what. This grit and creative energy set the Odesans apart.

The dynamism of the city, which attracted so many ethnicities, religions, and wealth, can be traced back to the nineteenth century when it became a *porto franco*, essentially a duty-free haven. From around that time Odesa started to grow rapidly also thanks to the lively trade in wheat. In fact, during the major refurbishment of the Odesa Opera House, grains of wheat, a bottle of red wine, and a registrar of the city's ledger were discovered in its foundation. This discovery speaks volumes about the history and the character of Odesa.

Ukrainians, Jews, Greeks, Germans, French, Italians, Polish, Bulgarians, Romanians, Moldovans, Armenians, Georgians, Albanians, Gagauz, Tatars, and Russians are just some of the ethnicities that have made the multicultural broth of Odesa. Many streets bear names that reflect the cosmopolitan nature of the place, such as French Avenue, Bulgarian Street, a neighborhood called Moldovanka, Lutheran Lane, Polish Descend, Italian Boulevard, Big and Small Arnautskaya streets (Arnauts were the Christian Albanians). With so many nationalities living side by side here for centuries, Odesa has been both worldly and a universe of its own. No matter what religion you followed, how you dressed, what language or dialect you spoke, here you could do business, make art, set up a home—and feel like you belonged. No matter where we've come from, this city has become our home and we feel fiercely proud of it (even when making jokes about its shortcomings!).

OUR CULTURE AND VITALITY

Odesa is the third largest city in Ukraine, and you'll hear a multitude of languages spoken here and encounter people whose character is as unique as Odesa itself: full of joy, optimism, love of life, and a very special sense of humor. We have two favorite pastimes: to have a laugh and to eat.

All this mixing of languages and ethnicities sparked a sense of humor that really sets Odesa apart. Our humor is warm, self-deprecating, impossible to translate, and often based on acute human observations, all of which help to soften tensions that inevitably come up between people. The Odesan character is good-natured, open, and always willing to share (and sometimes overshare!). We like to dress well regardless of our income, to party, and of course, to eat good food.

If you visit Odesa during our high season—from May to September—the city will welcome you with bright sunshine, leafy green trees, the sweet aroma of white acacia, the annoying and cheerful crowds of tourists, and busy beaches with lots of restaurants and clubs right on the seafront. Odesa in season never sleeps. Odesans and visitors alike spend most of their time outdoors, be it lounging around on the terrace of a summerhouse by the sea, cooking in summer kitchens, or on the beach, and even sleeping on balconies and in gardens during the warmer months. This joie de vivre spreads like fire.

One place in Odesa where you can experience this vitality and the city's multicultural flavor is Privoz one of the oldest food markets, located close to the main train station. Producers from neighboring regions come here once or twice a week to bring their best produce and other food items: Bulgarian brynza (a feta-like cheese), Korean pickles, Armenian flatbread lavash, Ukrainian cured pork *salo*, German sausages, Jewish stuffed chicken neck, Georgian Suluguni cheese, Moldavian peppers, and wine made with local grapes using French techniques. Seasoned regulars—we call them "burnt" or "scorched"—come to the market on specific days to buy the ingredients from their favorite vendors. Relationships are built for life this way, passed on from hand to hand and from one generation to another.

OUR FOOD

I sometimes think that for Odesans, our life purpose is to "make a bazaar"—a local expression that refers to all the bantering, gossiping, and haggling that take place when buying food at a market. Food just doesn't taste as good if we eat alone, so we always invite others to join in: family, friends, passersby, neighbors. Whoever needs feeding. If you ask most Ukrainians why they visit Odesa, they are likely to answer, "to enjoy the sea and to eat!"

Many of our talented chefs are self-taught, having grown up on their mother's lap (and grandmother's and grandfather's), learning, slurping, tasting. Even during Soviet times, when options to eat outside the home were generally very limited, Odesa had plenty of eateries to choose from. And over the last twenty years, this number has increased exponentially, with Odesa becoming one of the culinary capitals of Ukraine, from the most basic eating joints to more elaborate restaurants. Many places now serve food that is steeped in tradition but modernized, often made with local ingredients. Odesa is an eternally chewing city.

Odesans generally prefer substance over style when it comes to food (although see my note on the Feasts of Odesa, page 292). Every time I come back to Odesa and to the Privoz Market, I am amazed by the quality and variety of produce. You can still buy ingredients grown or reared by primary producers, which has become such a privilege in many parts of the world. Eating in season is a given in Odesa; fermenting and canning when fruits and vegetables are in glut are still a regular practice. Come to someone's house at the height of the season and you'll see freshly filled jars with colorful, handwritten labels lined up on balconies and in cellars. Even the most sophisticated meal at a restaurant cannot compete with the food at home. Debates and arguments about which recipe is "correct" never cease. Everyone is right in their own way, and that in itself is what makes the Odesan cuisine so rich. Food is the topic you'll most likely encounter when people sit around the table or gather anywhere, full stop! We love talking about food.

ABOUT ME

I grew up in Moldovanka, a neighborhood near a train station called Odesa Malaya (Little Odesa) because my great-grandfather had been the head of the station. It was a very modest neighborhood, where everyone knew each other. I fell in love with food as a little girl because even though we didn't have much at home—my mum loved good food but didn't love cooking—I was blessed with having access to the best Odesan food thanks to our neighbors. I learned to expect certain dishes in each house: a honey cake at Aunty Beba's, borsch with beans at Aunty Lena's, barbecued *shashlik* at Uncle Gosha's. And no one could fry fish better than Uncle Fima. One of my first memories of really enjoying food is from when I was three years old. I was at the wake for our elderly neighbor and was given a plate of wild mushrooms fried with *smetana* (sour cream). I couldn't stop eating them! I still remember the sense of shame (I'm at a funeral!) and pleasure fusing in me while stuffing my mouth with the mushrooms!

The best cook in our family was my grandmother Marusya Grab, after whom I was named (Maria and Marusya are versions of the same name). She was known throughout our neighborhood because of her powerful and beautiful voice. During festivities Marusya always sang and people from neighboring *dvoriks* came by just to listen to her. In her younger years, she was supposed to be an opera singer at the Odesa Opera House, but she couldn't follow that path because she'd married a high-ranking communist (opera was considered to be an alien form of art by the communist party, too "Western").

My grandmother was a real Odesan beauty who loved clothes, hats, bags, and furs. I was forbidden to open her wardrobes, but of course, as a little girl, I never listened, opening those mysterious chests of treasures! With age, Marusya became a proper *Maman* who adored children and reveled in cooking. Marusya's borsch with fermented tomatoes, served with garlicky rye bread and exquisitely thin slivers of frozen *salo*, was legendary.

I didn't initially follow a career in food. Eventually my love of food led me to opening a cooking school, establishing Ukraine's first food and wine road, and founding Odesan and Bessarabian Tours. In 2014, I moved to London with my family, where the idea of writing this book was born.

ABOUT THIS BOOK

I am incredibly grateful to everyone who shared their recipes with me—especially since people in Odesa are very protective of them! There are two people I would like to thank separately for helping me bring this book to life. Felicity Spector, a British journalist and a food blogger who I met during a particularly difficult phase of the war. Her never-failing belief that the world had to know about Odesa's food culture and its people, her support throughout the whole process of making this book a reality, her love for Odesa, and her insatiable curiosity about the things I didn't think a non-Odesan would understand have all been a great inspiration to me, giving me strength to keep going when I didn't think I could.

The second person I want to thank is Katrina Kollegaeva, or Katya, a British food writer, anthropologist, and chef originally from Estonia, who has tackled the huge task of translating my love letter to Odesa into English. Katya knows Ukraine very well, having spent all her summers with her family there, as her mother was from a place very close to Odesa. So she and I have spent hours deliberating on which word or expression was best to use or how to convey the spirit of a particular family story.

While creating this book I was walking around my city, recording the fading beauty of its architecture, spending time in the kitchens of many Odesan families, and hungrily writing down their life histories. I really wanted to capture the story of our city before, possibly, it was too late. I wanted to show our diversity and what we call our *colorit*, a very particular Odesan vitality, our life force. I was trying to find an answer to the question of what was special about Odesa that we can never forget, no matter where we end up living. We insistently seek places and food that remind us of Odesa, we search for ways to replicate the flavors and memories of our childhood, to take us back to our happy (and not always happy) days.

There are so many stories and recipes we couldn't include in this book, but I will continue writing about Odesa's food and people—and our humor—on my Instagram page. I'd love for you to come and follow me.

35
30
1300
35
1030
25
13
25
10
6

12 Principles of Odesan Cuisine

1. Beauty is in everything, from the plate to the surroundings to the people who make and eat the food (beauty has endless permutations!). The use of quality ingredients is a given.

2. Food must be elegant, dainty (preferably finger-size!), and always require at least a little bit of an effort. Revealing your recipe's secret? Only on your deathbed. What makes Odesan cuisine unique is its nuances, which you need to earn—not just learn.

3. The table should be overflowing. Feel free to serve dishes in two or three tiers. In my childhood, in our tiny Soviet apartments, plates were balanced on multiple tables, even on top of cabinets and windowsills, and even in winter, outside on balconies.

4. From nose to tail, everything is edible—but you must make it delicious and look beautiful (see point 1).

5. There can never be too much fried onion!

6. Freshness is the key to the success of any fish dish. (Ideally, you would catch the fish yourself in the morning.)

7. Children should eat well—and eat a lot. So much so that the grandmother starts to see the lovely pudgy rolls of fat on the child's arms and legs.

8. During the summer, splash in the sea for as long as your soul desires, but whatever else happens, lunch must be exactly on schedule. Bring a picnic to the beach—that's nonnegotiable.

9. Can and ferment everything possible. Put all your summer produce into glass jars, as they'll come in handy during the colder months. During the winter, you should eat as deliciously and diversely as in the summer.

10. Food *is* medicine. If you think that yellow cherry *kompot* is just a drink, or chicken broth is just a soup, you're mistaken.

11. People go to the market for way more than just food. To haggle, to gossip, and to catch up with friends and vendors. If you haven't sampled everything and bargained for everything, you're definitely not from Odesa. Good traders are like antiques—they're passed down through generations.

12. If humanity has not yet created the right kitchenware for Odesan dishes, make them yourself. It doesn't matter if it's a simple wooden *sekachka* knife to prepare eggplant caviar or a large, multi-layered pot to cook one specific stuffed-fish recipe. On Malaya Arnautskaya Street, they're always up for manufacturing any tool you might need and for a reasonable price. After all, nothing is too much to ask when it comes to a gorgeous table display and making your favorite food taste extra special!

Odesan Ingredients

BLACK SEA FISH

It is difficult to imagine a holiday in Odesa without a meal that includes some delicious Black Sea fish (although we love to eat the fish from local rivers and estuaries too). We eat fish seasonally and some types are unique to this area, like Black Sea sprats. The white flesh with very few bones is a delicacy. In the past this small fish with tiny bones was the food of the poor—until they created lots of delectable Black Sea sprat dishes that the wealthy fell in love with it too. Then there is the king of our waters, flounder, also known as the Black Sea chicken, that you cannot miss if you come across it on menus at Odesan restaurants.

Every Odesan boy would have been to the piers to fish for gobies, hunt for the rachki shrimp, or collect mussels. You'll see men fishing along the sea line all the time. You can then buy some of this freshly caught fish directly from the fishermen if you come to one specific entrance of the Privoz Market.

ODESA BLACK

A unique variety of grape indigenous to this part of Ukraine, Odesa Black is smoky and chocolaty with bright berry notes and, as the name suggests, an intensely dark color. It was little known until a few years ago. I am proud to say that I realized the potential of Odesa Black a few years ago when I decided to organize a big event that kick-started a much wider interest in this wine variety, both within Ukraine and increasingly abroad.

Now over forty vineyards are growing this grape throughout Ukraine and lots of events showcase the wine. You can't beat a glass of Odesa Black with a tender piece of roasted Bessarabian lamb on a summer night.

YELLOW CHERRIES

There are times during the year that all Odesans look forward to, as they punctuate the year with bursts of deliciousness. One of those is the all-too-brief yellow cherry season. The fruit ripens all at once so the cherries need to be collected and processed quickly. They can't be frozen so you have to either eat them all or make a jam or something even more popular, a *kompot*—a slightly sweetened drink with whole cherries preserved in the liquid. This *kompot* is not just a delicacy but considered a potent medicine, especially good for children's immunity. You'll see lots of cherry trees growing across Odesa. Many were left undisturbed when the old buildings were taken down to be replaced with new housing. I am proud of the wise people who left these trees untouched. They add so much beauty, color, and flavor to the city. Wilderness on your doorstep.

MIKADO TOMATOES

In the south of Ukraine we eat a lot of tomatoes and know lots of varieties, many of which are heritage. In Odesa, the Mikado is the king of them all. It has a delicate, thin skin and a perfectly balanced sweet-and-sour flavor. This huge, rosy-red specimen can weigh up to 21 to 25 oz (600 to 700 g) and can be a meal in itself. The Mikado is notoriously difficult to grow. The plant is prone to disease, with tomatoes of different sizes growing from the bottom to the top very fast. To protect the fruits at the bottom, they get smeared with clay over one side to prevent cracking. Otherwise, they would go bad before they ripen. So growing a Mikado is a labor of love.

I have kept a notebook for ten years of all the people who grow this tomato in and around Odesa. Whenever I see a seller of a genuine Mikado tomato (there are many fake ones on sale), I'd buy the lot and record the producer's number. People often don't realize the true value of growing such a majestic tomato and so don't want to pay for it, but we'll lose it if we don't keep up the production. I'm determined to keep the Mikado alive.

RODNICHOK CUCUMBERS

I should start by saying that cucumbers are a very important part of our food culture. We eat them throughout the year in many different ways, both raw and fermented. If you have only tried the long, smooth, and less flavorful variety that is predominant in the UK and the United States, you won't know what a delicacy a truly delicious, crunchy, fresh cucumber can be! Rodnichok is an indigenous Ukrainian variety of small cucumbers. Pale green, with tender little "pimples," it is unbelievably delicious with a balanced, almost sweet taste and a very thin skin that you'd be a fool to peel.

Rodnichoks are very seasonal (and not normally grown in greenhouses), quite pricey, and much treasured. Vendors lay them out in boxes as if they are jewelry or some expensive fruit. For a few precious weeks, you'll see old men or women by the side of the roads selling these cucumbers in small quantities, carefully laid out, or "kissed," as we like to say, in wide bowls or baskets with their flowers still intact. The root of the name Rodnichok means belonging to your family or your country, something close to your heart and soul. I love these little cucumbers very much.

DILL

To Ukrainians, what basil is to Italians or what cilantro leaves are to Thai people, as we use dill extensively in so many dishes. Borsch without dill is unimaginable and many recipes in this book include dill. But we don't use only the tender, fresh sprigs of the herb. The offshoots of overgrown dill plants, the so-called "dill umbrellas" (the thick stems look like the most adorable little umbrellas), are essential for fermenting cucumbers and other vegetables. We also dry and freeze fresh dill. In old southern Ukrainian kitchens you'll see bunches of dill, red hot peppers, and garlic hanging from the ceiling close to the oven to dry, as if they are some kind of aromatic lanterns. This herb is extremely good for you too. Odesan cuisine hasn't been studied as widely as the Mediterranean (yet!), but I'm sure we'll discover the medicinal properties of dill soon enough. For now, do as Ukrainians do and fall in love with this mildly aniseed-flavored wonder-herb.

SUNFLOWER SEEDS AND OIL

Sunflower oil to a Ukrainian is what olive oil is to a Greek—we eat it all day, every day, for its flavor and smell, especially if we move abroad to remind us of home. Unlike extra-virgin olive oil, it's not easy to get hold of good Ukrainian unrefined sunflower oil. The standard stuff you see in supermarkets has very little to do with our highly aromatic unrefined sunflower oil, which is a deep, dark amber color.

There are two types of sunflower oil in Ukraine: one made with raw sunflower seeds and the other with roasted seeds. The former is used for cooking as it's very mild in flavor and withstands high heat. The latter is used to dress salads and to finish dishes. I can't imagine our eggplant caviar without it.

Traditionally we had communal mills where people from neighboring villages would bring their seeds to extract the oil. This still happens in some rural areas. I grew up next to a factory that produced sunflower oil and loved the strong aroma. Now that I live far away from Odesa, I always carry a bottle of unrefined oil with me, treasured for the few dishes where you just can't replace the flavor, like a simple summer tomato salad (see page 79).

BRYNZA CHEESE

Brynza is our most popular and best-loved type of cheese. It can be made from cow's or sheep's milk or a mix of the two. In Bessarabia people prefer the saltier and more intense sheep milk's version, but in Odesa we hanker after what we call "sweet brynza"—a delicate, creamy version made with cow's milk. Its flavor is somewhat similar to mozzarella, with a crumbly texture rather like feta, but brynza is really its own beautiful thing. Odesans like to buy brynza in small rounds and eat it within a day or two, then buy more once it's finished. Crusty bread with a thick layer of freshly churned butter and a slice of brynza, alongside a cup of sweet black tea, is the best breakfast you can imagine.

A few years ago I organized a panel discussion in Odesa about our local ingredients including, of course, brynza cheese. Among the panelists were two foreign chefs, one from Italy and another from France. I asked them why they chose to live and work in Odesa. After all, they came from countries famed for the quality of their fresh produce, cheese, and other foods. "Tomatoes and brynza," they replied in unison.

On a Sunny Morning

BREAKFASTS AND BITES

Placinta Flatbread

Placinta Savory or Sweet Flatbread

Andrej Velichko, a chef who now lives in Prague, is originally from Odesa. He worked in Odesan restaurants for a decade, modernizing the cuisine by incorporating elements of fine dining. He's a real expert on everything to do with Odesa's food and makes the most wonderful spice mixes based on Bessarabian traditions. Here he has chosen a recipe close to his heart—placinta, a type of flatbread that can be filled with all kinds of delicious ingredients. The one with cheese and dill is his favorite, but all three are special. It's exactly the sort of simple food prepared with plenty of care and attention that Andrej likes to champion.

DOUGH

18 oz (500 g) all-purpose flour, plus more for dusting

1 teaspoon sea salt

2 tablespoons sunflower oil, plus more for drizzling and cooking

About ¾ cup (6 fl oz/185 ml) water

COTTAGE CHEESE FILLING

1 bunch fresh dill

21 oz (600 g) cottage cheese

3½ oz (100 g) aged sheep's milk cheese, such as Ukrainian brynza cheese

1 egg

Sea salt

POTATO FILLING

25 oz (700 g) potatoes

4¼ oz (120 g) onions

1 tablespoon sunflower oil

Sea salt and freshly ground pepper

APPLE FILLING

6 small Golden Delicious apples

1¾ oz (50 g) sugar

2 tablespoons (10 g) cornstarch

Juice of ½ lemon

Confectioners' sugar for sprinkling

MAKES 10 FLATBREADS

To prepare the dough, in a large bowl, combine the flour and the salt. In a small bowl, mix the sunflower oil into the water, then pour this mixture into the flour and salt. Stir gently with a spoon and then knead with your hands until a rough dough forms. Lightly flour a work surface, transfer the dough to the floured surface, and continue kneading until the dough becomes smooth and elastic and no longer sticks to your hands. Wrap it in plastic wrap and let rest at room temperature for 20 minutes.

Divide the dough into 10 equal portions. Lightly dust each piece with flour and shape into a ball. Cover with plastic wrap and let rest again for 10 minutes.

To prepare the cottage cheese filling, finely chop the dill. In a large bowl, mash together the cottage cheese and brynza cheese with a fork. Add the egg, season with salt, and mix well, then stir in the dill until combined.

To prepare the potato filling, peel and coarsely grate the potatoes into a large bowl. Finely chop the onions and mix them into the potatoes along with the sunflower oil. Season with salt and pepper.

To prepare the apple filling, coarsely grate the apples into a large bowl, then add the sugar, cornstarch, and lemon juice and mix until combined.

Roll out a dough ball into a circle about 1⁄16 inch (2 mm) thick and 10 inches (25 cm) in diameter. Drizzle 1 tablespoon sunflower oil onto the rolled-out dough and use your hands to spread it evenly. Place the filling (either potato or apple) in the center and spread it evenly with a silicone spatula, leaving a border ¾ inch (2 cm) from the edge. Gently stretch the dough outward all the way around, then fold the four sides toward the center to form an envelope. Repeat the process by folding in the four corners of the square-shaped envelope. Finally, roll out the flatbread again with a rolling pin to seal the edges and make it thinner. Repeat with the remaining dough and filling.

Line a plate with paper towels. Pour sunflower oil into a large frying pan to a depth of ⅜ inch (1 cm) and heat over low heat until hot. Place a flatbread, seam-side down, in the pan and fry for 3 to 5 minutes, or until golden brown. Flip the flatbread, cover the pan with a lid, and fry for 3 to 4 minutes more. Transfer the flatbread to the paper towel–lined plate to absorb any excess oil. Repeat to fry the remaining flatbread. They are at their best served immediately. For the flatbreads with sweet fillings, sprinkle with confectioners' sugar before serving.

Finger-Size Pancakes with Curd Cheese

This recipe was passed on to Olya by her mother, Leonida, who was originally from the Vinnitsa region in central Ukraine and came to Odesa for love—Olya's dad. Making these tiny pancakes was an activity that involved the whole family. Olya has fond memories of spending afternoons "helping" her mum assemble these pancakes. Her mum wouldn't trust her with the delicate rolling process, but young Olya loved sitting there by her mum's side, singing and listening to stories. There's a tradition in Odesa of elaborate and minuscule dishes—"just one bite!" we often say. The more intricate and labor-intensive, the better. Often making such dishes, like these pancakes, would be an excuse for a celebration in itself. Now Olya carries on the tradition with her own daughter.

PANCAKES

8 eggs

1 tablespoon sugar

½ teaspoon sea salt

1 tablespoon sunflower oil, plus more for cooking

7 oz (200 g) all-purpose flour

2½ oz (70 g) cornstarch

About 1 quart (34 fl oz/1 l) whole milk

FILLING

24½ oz (700 g) full-fat curd cheese (recipe follows, page 28)

3½ oz (100 g) sugar

2 eggs

Seeds from 1 vanilla bean or 1 teaspoon vanilla paste

4¼ oz (120 g) raisins (optional)

3 oz (90 g) butter

SERVES 8–10

To prepare the pancakes, in a large bowl, whisk together the eggs, sugar, and salt until well combined. Add the sunflower oil and mix thoroughly. Gradually sift in the flour and cornstarch, stirring continuously until the batter is smooth. Slowly pour in the milk in a thin stream, whisking constantly to maintain a smooth consistency. The batter should be quite liquid.

Heat an 8½-inch (22-cm) nonstick frying pan over medium heat and lightly grease it with sunflower oil. Pour about one-third of a ladle of batter into the pan for each pancake, tilting the pan to spread the batter evenly; do not crowd the pan. Once the pancake begins to set, pour any remaining batter in the pan back into the bowl. As you cook, stir the batter occasionally. Fry each pancake for 1 to 2 minutes on each side, or until it turns pale yellow (don't let it get golden brown as the pancakes cook more in the oven). Flip with a spatula, then transfer to a plate, stacking the thin pancakes on top of each other.

To prepare the filling, in a medium bowl, mix together the curd cheese, sugar, eggs, and vanilla until smooth. Stir in the raisins (if using) and combine well.

Preheat the oven to 350°F (180°C).

Melt the butter in a small saucepan over medium heat. Grease a 10-inch (26-cm) round baking dish or ceramic mold with some of the melted butter. Place the stack of pancakes on a cutting board and, using a sharp knife, cut them into 4 equal pieces to form triangles.

Place 1 teaspoon of the filling on the wider end of each triangle. Roll the pancake once from the end with the filling, then fold in the sides and continue rolling until you have a tight roll about the size of your little finger. Place the pancakes, seam-side down, in the prepared baking dish to form a single layer, then brush with melted butter. Repeat with a second layer and brush the layer with butter.

Cover the mold with aluminum foil to prevent the pancakes from drying out. Bake for 30 to 40 minutes and serve warm.

Finger-Size Pancakes with Curd Cheese

Homemade Curd Cheese

Homemade Curd Cheese

Curd cheese, or *syr*, is one of those fundamental products that we Odesans eat almost daily. In my beloved Privoz Market, you will come across several tables dedicated just to this product (plus sometimes milk or butter). You can choose the level of saltiness and moisture you want in your cheese. Really good *syr* is naturally sweet and doesn't keep well, so we like to eat it within a couple of days. If you can't (yet!) visit the Privoz Market, I suggest you make the cheese at home. Get the best milk you can and follow this straightforward recipe. It's the closest you can get to experiencing the taste of Odesa at home.

About 2 quarts (68 fl oz/2 l) whole milk

10½ oz (300 g) organic natural yogurt or kefir

MAKES ABOUT 12½ OZ (350 G)

If using the oven method below, make sure the saucepan is oven-safe. Pour the milk into a large saucepan, add the yogurt, and mix well. Set the pan over medium heat and heat until it reaches 104°F (40°C). Cover the pan and let stand in a warm place for 24 hours or up to 2 days; the timing will depend on the temperature of your room. The soured milk should look like Greek yogurt when it's ready.

STOVETOP METHOD

Using a double boiler or bain-marie, half-fill the bottom pan with water and place the saucepan with the soured milk over the water (make sure the water does not touch the bottom of the saucepan). Set over low heat and begin heating the soured milk very slowly. Bring the water to a boil and simmer the milk for 1 hour, or until the whey separates from the cream and you can see thick cracks forming along the sides. Remove from the heat and let stand undisturbed until the milk cools to room temperature.

OVEN METHOD

Preheat the oven to 225°F (105°C). Place the covered saucepan with the soured milk in the oven. Bake for 40 to 60 minutes, or until the whey starts to separate from the curd. Remove the saucepan from the oven and let it cool to room temperature.

Line a fine-mesh sieve with a muslin cloth and set over a large bowl, then drain the curds for 1 hour. To form the curd cheese, gather the muslin into a bundle and gently squeeze out the remaining liquid. If you prefer drier curd cheese, weigh it in a muslin bundle for 1 to 2 more hours. Don't throw away the whey; you can use it to make pancakes. Put the curd cheese in a covered container and store in the fridge for up to 1 week. Serve the curd cheese with sour cream and honey or jam, or use it to prepare Felix's Favorite Curd Cheese Syrniki (page 29) or Lazy Dumplings (page 34).

Felix's Favorite Curd Cheese Syrniki

This recipe comes from me or, to be precise, from my Ukrainian grandma, Marusya. She loved to cook and was famous in our Moldovanka neighborhood for her beautiful and powerful voice. I still have a photo of her parents, more than a century old, which she kept in the all-important "icon" corner of her house. Marusya came from a prosperous and proud Cossack family with a surname Grab who had lost their fortunes during the Soviet Revolution.

In this photo you can see my great-grandmother (on the left) wearing plenty of golden jewelry, which the family had to exchange for food during the Second World War. But they kept one golden necklace, which Marusya passed on to me. That necklace is my reminder that food is more important than gold. Syrniki is also one of my son Felix's favorite dishes. That's why I spent many hours perfecting this recipe, although to be honest, the most important secret to great syrniki is using great Odesan curd cheese.

18 oz (500 g) full-fat curd cheese (page 28)

2 eggs

1 tablespoon superfine (caster) sugar

Sea salt

Seeds from 1 vanilla bean or 1 teaspoon vanilla paste

3 tablespoons all-purpose flour, plus more for dusting and dredging

½ teaspoon baking powder

3 oz (90 g) raisins

½ cup (4 fl oz/120 ml) sunflower oil

Honey, fresh berries, and sour cream

SERVES 6–8

The curd cheese should be as dry as possible. If needed, gently press it with a paper towel to remove the excess moisture. It should still hold its shape.

In a large bowl, combine the curd cheese, eggs, sugar, ½ teaspoon salt, and the vanilla. Mix thoroughly until the mixture is smooth. Add the flour and baking powder, then mix again. Fold in the raisins and mix gently until evenly distributed.

Pour some flour onto a deep plate. Dust your hands with flour. Roll about 1 tablespoon of the cheese mixture into a ball, dredge it lightly in the flour, and flatten with the palm of your hand to form a round pancake about ¾ inch (2 cm) thick and 1½ inches (4 cm) in diameter. Place the pancake on a floured board.

Heat the sunflower oil in a large frying pan over low heat. When the oil is hot and working in batches if needed, fry the pancakes for 2 to 3 minutes, then flip the pancakes, cover the pan with a lid, and fry the pancakes on the other side for 2 to 3 minutes. Serve the pancakes warm with honey, fresh berries, and sour cream.

NOTE

You can find excellent curd cheese or cottage cheese in Polish stores. Choose the one with the highest fat content to make the most tender syrniki pancakes. For a savory version, omit the raisins, sugar, and vanilla ingredients and serve the pancakes with smoked salmon, roasted tomatoes, or other savory toppings.

Felix's Favorite Curd Cheese Syrniki

Lazy Dumplings

Lazy Dumplings

Now a Londoner, Angelina was born in Odesa into a food-obsessed family. Even her packed school lunches included elaborate sandwiches filled with all sorts of delicious things. Spoiled by her mother's cooking with these intricate, homemade concoctions, Angelina recalls being desperate to be able to enjoy the school's basic canteen food. Such irony. As she grew up, she wanted to become a chef but also loved visual arts, so Angelina combined her two passions and became a food photographer.

For this book Angelina chose a classic Ukrainian recipe that relies on a light touch and good ingredients. These dumplings are called "lazy" because there's a more labor-intensive version (see page 195) that involves rolling out the dough separately and then filling it, but these lazy ones are just as delicious. You can use any good ricotta cheese here in place of the curd cheese, but make sure you drain it well and add a bit more flour to the mixture to hold it together.

9 oz (250 g) full-fat curd cheese (page 28)

Zest of 1 lemon

1 egg yolk

1 tablespoon superfine (caster) sugar

¼ cup (40 g) all-purpose flour, plus more for dusting

Sea salt

About 1 tablespoon butter

2 tablespoons sour cream

SERVES 2–3

In a bowl, combine the curd cheese, lemon zest, egg yolk, sugar, flour, and a pinch of salt. Mix everything together by hand until smooth, then shape into a large ball.

Dust a work surface with flour. Transfer the dough to the surface and divide into 3 equal pieces. Roll each piece into a "sausage" shape, lightly dusting it with flour to prevent sticking. Cut the dough into small, free-form pieces to create the lazy dumplings.

Bring a large saucepan of water to a boil over high heat and add a pinch of salt. Once it comes to a rolling boil, throw in the dumplings and immediately stir so they don't stick to the bottom. Once the dumplings float to the surface, reduce the heat and simmer for 2 to 3 minutes more.

Carefully drain the dumplings in a colander and transfer them to a large bowl. Add the butter to the hot dumplings, then gently shake the bowl to coat them evenly. Avoid stirring with a spoon so the dumplings will keep their shape. Serve the dumplings topped with a spoonful of sour cream.

NOTE

You could even garnish lazy dumplings with honeycomb and mint or fresh berries for an extra-special dessert.

Chopped Chicken Liver and Pork Belly Pâté

There's one very famous *dvorik* courtyard in Odesa, located at Dovolanovskij Spusk 1, where city guides bring visitors to show them what a real *dvorik* looks like. You must come and see it when you get to visit Odesa! In fact, I hope that by the time this book is out, I'll be able to organize pop-up feasts in that very courtyard. You've got to experience the real community feeling, to hear crickets chirping, the sounds of the city at night, how people sing and hold loud debates—usually about food—and argue with each other around the table.

There's one person in this *dvorik* whose name is Lyubov (the name that literally means Love) who holds the fabric of the entire community together. She takes care of the elderly, gives advice to the young, and even looks after all the pets and plants whenever she's needed. Lyubov has worked in the Odesan port all her life. When she was young, she was tempted to leave Odesa in search of a better life—like many people did at the time. But when she reached the airport, she realized there was no way she could leave her *dvorik* and her home in Odesa. She stayed and never looked back. In Lyubov's *dvorik* there were debates about the way to make this pâté, and all agreed her recipe was the best. Since then, she always makes this dish for all the *dvorik* feasts.

18 oz (500 g) chicken livers

12½ oz (350 g) pork belly

About 3½ tablespoons sunflower oil

2 onions

1 large carrot

Sea salt and freshly ground pepper

SERVES 10

Cut the chicken livers and pork belly into large cubes, roughly equal in size. Heat the sunflower oil in a large, heavy-bottomed saucepan over medium heat. Add the pork belly and fry until golden brown.

Peel and cut the onions into large pieces, then add them to the pork belly in the pan and fry for 10 minutes. Peel and cut the carrot into large cubes, add them to the pan, and fry for 10 minutes. Add the chicken livers, mix everything well, and cover with a lid. Simmer for 10 minutes. Season with salt and pepper, cover, and continue simmering for 10 to 15 minutes more.

Using a meat grinder or a food processor, grind the ingredients together into a paste. Store in a jar in the fridge for up to 3 days. The pâté can also be frozen for up to 3 months.

NOTE

In Odesa, this pâté is usually spread on bread and served with fresh Rodnichok cucumbers, which are very crisp and sweet, from the Privoz Market.

Chopped Chicken Liver and Pork Belly Pâté

Pumpkin and Milk Porridge

Pumpkin and Milk Porridge

It's difficult to catch Lena in her kitchen, as she is a busy businesswoman and travels a lot, but there are certain dishes that Lena always makes at home at certain times of the year, no matter what. This pumpkin porridge is one of them. Get the best pumpkin you can find, as the final result is all about the pumpkin flavor. Lena always buys hers from the same lady at the market. Here in Odesa, families pass on their knowledge about the best vendors like a kind of "inheritance" in Odesa, from one generation to another! This combination of rice and pumpkin is a childhood favorite for many Ukrainians.

1 pumpkin, about 1½ lb (700 g)

About 1 cup (7 fl oz/200 ml) water

7 oz (200 g) short-grain white rice

About 3½ cups (27 fl oz/800 ml) whole milk

1¾ oz (50 g) superfine (caster) sugar

Sea salt

1¾ oz (50 g) butter

SERVES 4

Peel the pumpkin and scoop out the seeds. Cut the pumpkin flesh into ½-inch (12-mm) cubes. Transfer the pumpkin to a large saucepan and add the water to cover. Bring to a boil over medium heat, then simmer for about 10 minutes, or until the pumpkin is soft. Add the rice, milk, sugar, and salt and mix well.

Simmer the porridge over low heat for 15 minutes, or until the rice is just tender. Add the butter and mix well. Remove from the heat, cover with a lid, and let the porridge stand for 10 to 15 minutes before serving.

Shakshuka the Odesan Way

Misha Reva is a well-known artist and sculptor in Ukraine. One of his works, a door opening onto the Black Sea (you have to see its magic to understand!), is called *The House of Sun*, which is what many locals call Odesa. Misha has a *dacha* (summerhouse) by the sea where he often makes this famous egg dish. He calls it "with everything" because he changes up the ingredients depending on the season and what's at hand. This version is particularly special to him because the fresh walnuts give the dish a creamy, milky dimension.

1 red onion

2 cloves garlic

6 small tomatoes

1¾ oz (50 g) walnut pieces

4 spring onions

4 fresh dill sprigs

1¾ oz (50 g) butter

5½ oz (150 g) smoked bacon lardons

8 eggs

Sea salt and freshly ground pepper

Sourdough bread

SERVES 4

Peel and finely chop the red onion and garlic. Cut the tomatoes into quarters. Chop the walnuts into small pieces. Chop the spring onions and dill.

Melt the butter in a large frying pan over low heat. Add the lardons and fry until translucent. Add the red onion and garlic and sauté, stirring occasionally, until golden brown. Add the tomatoes, cover the pan with a lid, and simmer briefly until the tomatoes soften and release their juices.

Crack the eggs one at a time into the pan, spacing them evenly apart. Season with salt and pepper and sprinkle the walnuts on top. Cover the pan and cook for 5 to 7 minutes, or until the egg whites are just set but the yolks are still runny. Sprinkle with the spring onions and dill. Remove from the heat and serve immediately with slices of white bread.

SALVE

Shakshuka the Odesan Way

Grandma's Crepes

Grandma's Crepes

Natasha is an art and fashion historian and a long-term resident of Prague. Like many Odesan children, she was often sent to stay with her grandparents for holidays. Far away from the hustle and bustle of Odesa, Natasha indulged in the pleasures of village life: sleeping on feather quilts, waking up to roosters crowing, drinking milk fresh from a cow's udder, and enjoying these crepes straight from the stove. This recipe has been made by four generations of Natasha's family, and now Natasha is teaching her daughter how to prepare them. Since its humble beginnings, the recipe has been changed and transformed, but Natasha and I have restored it to its original form. You can eat the crepes with a generous serving of honey or sweetened curd cheese or, on major holidays, with red caviar.

3 eggs

3 tablespoons superfine (caster) sugar

Sea salt

2 tablespoons sunflower oil, plus more for cooking

9 oz (250 g) all-purpose flour

About 2 cups (17 fl oz/500 ml) whole milk

1¾ oz (50 g) butter

MAKES 14 CREPES

In a large bowl, beat together the eggs, sugar, and a pinch of salt until smooth. Add the sunflower oil and flour and mix thoroughly to prevent any lumps. Pour in the milk and mix until smooth. Let the batter rest at room temperature for 30 minutes.

Heat an 8½-inch (22-cm) nonstick frying pan over medium heat and lightly grease it with sunflower oil. Pour half a ladle of batter into the pan and spread it evenly. Cook the crepe, flipping once with a spatula, for 1 to 2 minutes on each side, or until golden brown. Transfer each crepe to a serving plate and rub it with a cube of butter on a fork. Repeat with the remaining batter, greasing the pan with more oil as needed and rubbing each finished crepe with butter.

Cheese Zakuska from the Queen of Moldovanka

Yulya, who provided this recipe, has a classic story, from riches to rags . . . and back to riches. In Ukraine she is a very well-known writer with numerous accolades. Her book *Odesan Saga* tells a multigenerational story of a Jewish family living in a quintessential *dvorik*, or courtyard, in a Moldovanka neighborhood, a kind of *dvorik* where Yulya herself grew up. The books became so popular that Yulya has been given a moniker, "the queen of Moldovanka."

But in 2022 Yulya had to leave her life behind when she migrated to the United States with her family to start all over again: from cleaning in a care home to publishing a newspaper and to running a successful business creating decorations for events. Yulya still writes, of course, being inspired and not trodden by her new life. She will forever carry a piece of Odesa and its *dvoriks* within her, where the simplest of foods is made with creativity and love, carrying the spirit of generosity no matter where you end up living.

3½ oz (100 g) Gouda or similar cheese

3½ oz (100 g) Cheddar or similar cheese

3 cloves garlic

About ⅔ cup (5 fl oz/150 ml) mayonnaise

Freshly ground pepper

White sourdough or plain éclairs (optional)

SERVES 6

Coarsely grate the cheeses into a bowl. Press the garlic through a garlic press into the bowl. Add the mayonnaise and pepper to taste and mix well.

If using éclairs, cut a small slit on the side of each one. Using a teaspoon, fill the éclairs with the zakuska. Serve the filled éclairs chilled. If not using éclairs, serve the zakuska with sourdough bread.

Cheese Zakuska from the Queen of Moldovanka

Crispy Zucchini Fritters

Crispy Zucchini Fritters and Cabbage Fritters

Iness has French roots and owns the Blossom Space, a stunning venue that combines French style with Odesa's spirit. Before opening the space in Odesa, she and her mother traveled together around France, spending much of their time in Provence. Iness's mother, Natalie, was taught by her father how to notice and capture the essence of beauty, whether it's a snowflake, a leaf, or piece of fabric on a table. Natalie has passed on this ability to her daughter, and this dish is a case in point—you can find versions of it all over Eastern Europe, often made with large zucchini at the end of the summer season. You have to take your time when frying these fritters. They need to be crisp but cooked through on the inside. Iness serves them with a garlicky sour cream sauce, and I encourage you to do likewise.

ZUCCHINI FRITTERS

1 zucchini

1 teaspoon superfine (caster) sugar

Sea salt

2 cloves garlic

1 egg

3 tablespoons all-purpose flour

5 tablespoons (2½ fl oz/75 ml) sunflower oil

3½ oz (100 g) sour cream

CABBAGE FRITTERS

10½ oz (300 g) young cabbage (preferably sweetheart cabbage)

Sea salt

A handful of chopped fresh dill

2 eggs

¼ cup (1 oz/30 g) all-purpose flour

3 tablespoons sunflower oil, plus more as needed

3½ oz (100 ml) sour cream

EACH RECIPE SERVES 4

To make the zucchini fritters, grate the zucchini, transfer to a bowl, and add the sugar and salt. Incorporate the sugar and salt with your hands. Set aside for 10 minutes to give the salt time to draw the moisture from the zucchini.

Place the zucchini in a colander and squeeze out as much liquid as you can with your hands. Then transfer the zucchini to a kitchen towel and squeeze again until you can't wring out any more liquid. You might need to use a second towel. Place the zucchini in a bowl. Press the garlic through a garlic press, then add the garlic and the egg to the bowl and mix well. Add the flour and mix again.

Line a plate with paper towels. Heat the sunflower oil in a large frying pan over medium heat. When the oil is hot and working in batches if needed, add 1 tablespoon of the batter to make each pancake. Fry for 2 to 3 minutes on each side, or until golden brown. Transfer the pancakes to the paper towel–lined plate to absorb any excess oil. Serve with the sour cream.

To make the cabbage fritters, finely shred the cabbage as thinly as possible, transfer to a bowl, and add salt. Press the cabbage firmly with your hands. The longer you press down on the cabbage, the more tender the pancakes will be. Add the dill and eggs to the bowl and mix well. Add the flour and mix again.

Line a plate with paper towels. Heat the sunflower oil in a large frying pan over medium heat. When the oil is hot and working in batches if needed, add 1 tablespoon of the batter to make each pancake. Fry for 1 to 2 minutes on each side, or until golden brown. While frying the pancakes, keep adding a little more oil to the pan so it doesn't become dry. Transfer the pancakes to the paper towel–lined plate to absorb any excess oil. Serve with the sour cream.

NOTE
In-season zucchini are usually less watery, so they don't need to be squeezed out as thoroughly.

Sweet Eggy Bread Toast Hrenka

If you live in Ukraine and appreciate beautiful tableware, you'll probably be familiar with the work of Svitlana Sabri (@svsabri). Svitlana started the business out of her home, inspired by her love of quirky vintage plates and glasses. Now she lives in Paris, where she has continued to expand her range with French and other European pieces. Svitlana often makes her favorite childhood dish for breakfast—sweet toast hrenka, a version of the French *pain perdu*, often called French toast in English. She serves this simple dish with her characteristic chic—on porcelain plates with lacy linen napkins alongside. It's in the Odesan nature to make food both taste great and look beautiful!

2 eggs

Superfine (caster) sugar to taste

About 1 cup (7 fl oz/200 ml) whole milk

Butter for frying

6 slices white bread

Sea salt

Sour cream

Jam or fresh berries

SERVES 6

In a deep bowl, use a whisk or wooden spoon to beat together the eggs and sugar. Add the milk and mix until smooth.

Melt butter in a large frying pan over medium heat. Dip each slice of bread into the egg mixture for a few minutes, allowing it to soak thoroughly. Working in batches if needed, fry each slice on both sides until golden brown. Serve warm with a sprinkle of sea salt and a spoonful of sour cream and jam or berries.

Sweet Eggy Bread Toast Hrenka

Kefir Drop-Pancakes

Kefir Drop-Pancakes

Drop-pancakes are probably the most beloved dish of all Odesan children. They are a quintessential breakfast food that can also be "elevated" by making smaller ones for canapés. No need for those dull, store-bought blinis ever again! This recipe was given to us by Natasha, who is originally from Odesa but now lives full-time in Paris with her little daughter, Eva. As a proper Odesan child, Eva already loves food and cooking, even at her tender age of 4. When I first started working on this book, kefir was not a very widely known product, but now you can buy it in most supermarkets. Kefir is not only good for you but also makes these pancakes very light and airy.

About 1 cup (9 fl oz/250 ml) kefir

About 3½ tablespoons boiling water

1 egg

2 tablespoons superfine (caster) sugar

Sea salt

7 oz (200 g) all-purpose flour, plus more if needed

¼ teaspoon baking soda

7 tablespoons (3½ fl oz/100 ml) sunflower oil

SERVES 4–6

In a large bowl, combine the kefir and boiling water. In a small bowl, whisk together the egg, sugar, and ½ teaspoon salt. Add the egg mixture to the bowl with kefir and water. Add the flour and mix until the batter is smooth and thick like heavy cream. Add more flour if needed to achieve the right consistency. Finally, add the baking soda and mix well. Start frying the pancakes immediately.

Line a plate with paper towels. Pour the sunflower oil into a large frying pan to a depth of ¼ inch (6 mm) and heat over medium heat. When the oil is hot and working in batches if needed so you don't crowd the pan, drop in 1 tablespoon of the batter to make each pancake. Fry for 2 to 3 minutes on each side, or until crisp and golden brown. Transfer the pancakes to the paper towel–lined plate to absorb any excess oil.

NOTE

Odesan grandmothers serve these pancakes to their grandchildren with sour cream and honey or jam.

Sour Cherry Pies

Sour cherries have a very special place in the Ukrainian heart. These cherries are sweet and only a little bit sour; in fact, our name for them is *vyshnya*, which doesn't have the sour connotation. When traveling in the Odesan countryside, you'll see that each village has its own unique look; this is because each is populated by one predominant ethnicity. In front of every traditional Ukrainian village house, you'll always see a sour cherry tree, often painted white at the bottom to protect it from insects. Because cherries have a short season, everyone rushes to enjoy them while they last. Odesan kitchens are filled with the aroma of cherries, which are used to make pies, dumplings, compotes, jams, the legendary cherry liqueur, and even cherries preserved in their own juices—perfect for winter pies that bring back memories of sunny Odesan summers.

This recipe comes from a wife and husband duo, Oksana and Misha, who have a long-standing tradition of throwing a pie party every year during the sour cherry season, usually around June. These yeasted pies are the darlings of Ukrainian cuisine. They are made with a brioche-style dough, which means they are unbelievably light. Some might be fried, others are baked, but the plates with freshly made pies always get polished off the moment the hosts put them onto the table.

DOUGH

1⅓ teaspoons (4 g) fast-acting dried yeast

About 1 cup (9 fl oz/250 ml) lukewarm milk

18 oz (500 g) all-purpose flour

1 oz (30 g) superfine (caster) sugar

3½ oz (100 g) unsalted butter, at room temperature

1 tablespoon sunflower oil

1 medium egg

Sea salt

SOUR CHERRIES

2 lb (1 kg) sour cherries

2¾ oz (80 g) superfine (caster) sugar

About ⅔ cup (5 fl oz/150 ml) sunflower oil

2½ oz (70 g) confectioners' sugar

MAKES 30 MINI PIES

To make the dough, in a small bowl, whisk the yeast into warm milk along with about 1 oz (25 g) of the flour and the superfine sugar until smooth. Let rest in a warm place until it becomes bubbly and rises.

Meanwhile in a large bowl, combine the remaining flour, the butter, sunflower oil, egg, and ½ teaspoon salt. Pour in the risen yeast mixture and knead the dough until it becomes smooth and elastic. Do not add any more flour. Transfer the dough to a lightly oiled bowl, cover with plastic wrap, and let rise in a warm place for 1½ to 2 hours, or until doubled in size.

To make the sour cherries, pit the cherries and place them in a colander to drain off any excess juice. Knead the dough and divide it into 30 equal pieces. Shape each piece into a small ball, cover with plastic wrap, and let rest for 15 minutes.

Lightly oil your hands and a work surface. Roll out each dough ball into a 3¼-inch (8-cm) circle about ¼ inch (5 mm) thick. Place ½ teaspoon of the superfine sugar and 3 cherries in the center of each circle, fold over the filled circle into a half-moon, and then pinch the edges tightly to seal.

Line a plate with paper towels. Pour the sunflower oil into a large, deep frying pan to a depth of ⅜ inch (1 cm) and heat over medium heat. Working in batches as needed, fry the pies, flipping once, until golden brown on both sides. Transfer the pies to the paper towel–lined plate to absorb any excess oil. Place the pies on a serving plate and sprinkle with confectioners' sugar.

Sour Cherry Pies

Summerhouse Food

SALADS AND VEGETABLES

Piquant Fried Zucchini

Piquant Fried Zucchini

Victoriya, whose recipe this is, has a large extended family that she spoils rotten. Many of them now live in different countries, but last year they gathered in one house for the all-important New Year's celebration. As she did for every family gathering, Victoriya had worked on the menu for weeks, even bringing some special ingredients from Odesa, frozen and carefully vacuum-packed.

Victoriya acquired her cooking skills by osmosis, simply by growing up in a family that worshipped food. Both her mother, Alla, and her grandmother Lyubov loved big feasts. The granny even had a team of women who used to come and help with the cooking! An impressive catering operation. No one in the family ate out, as restaurant food couldn't even come close to the deliciousness served at home. To this day in Victoriya's family, all celebrations are marked with home-cooked food around a (very big!) dining table. Victoriya takes time to pick out plates, tablecloths, and flowers to create a theme for each occasion depending on the time of year. Odesan feasts can make almost everything seem all right.

2 zucchini

Sea salt

5 tablespoons all-purpose flour

½ cup (4 fl oz/120 ml) sunflower oil

SAUCE

½ small bunch fresh dill

4 large cloves garlic

Sea salt

½ cup (4 fl oz/120 ml) water

3 tablespoons cider vinegar

SERVES 4–6

Slice the zucchini into rounds about ¼ inch (6 mm) thick. Place the slices in a bowl, sprinkle with salt, and mix well.

Pour the flour onto a plate. Dredge each zucchini slice in the flour, coating both sides and shaking off any excess. Set aside on a plate.

Line another plate with paper towels. Heat the sunflower oil in a large frying pan over high heat. Fry the zucchini slices on both sides until golden brown. Transfer the zucchini to the paper towel–lined plate to absorb any excess oil.

To make the sauce, finely chop the dill. Press the garlic through a garlic press. In a small bowl, combine the dill, garlic, ½ teaspoon salt, the water, and vinegar and mix well.

Place the warm zucchini slices in a single layer on a serving dish. Drizzle the sauce evenly over the slices, ensuring each one is covered.

Young Wild Garlic Salad

Wild garlic is one of the first signs that spring has come in the south of Ukraine. During the so-called "hungry gap" when very little produce is left from the previous year, and before the new season's vegetables appear, you can find big bunches of wild garlic at local markets. The first opportunity for *vitaminchiki*! The garlic grows wild in many places in and around Odesa and in the UK too; you can forage for these bright green, flat leaves quite easily if you know the places to look. This recipe comes from Yulya, the beautiful mom of Nika Lozovska (a young Odesan chef whose own recipe is on page 147). Yulya is from a Jewish family, where food played a really important role—mealtimes were always generous, delicious, and elegant. Versions of this recipe are made all over Odesa at this time of the year with the very delicate, almost creamy, new season's radishes, which are a must.

3 eggs
10½ oz (300 g) radishes
3 small cucumbers
7 oz (200 g) young wild garlic
4¼ oz (125 g) sour cream
Sea salt

SERVES 4–6

Put the eggs into a saucepan of cold water and bring to a boil over high heat. As soon as the water comes to a rolling boil, reduce the heat to low and set a timer for 7 minutes. When the time is up, drain the eggs and submerge them in cold water. Peel the eggs, then cut them into small cubes. Slice the radishes and cucumbers into thin half-moons. Finely chop the garlic.

In a large bowl, combine the eggs, radishes, cucumbers, and garlic. Add the sour cream and season with salt. Gently mix everything together until well combined. Serve in a beautiful crystal bowl for a touch of elegance.

Young Wild Garlic Salad

Spring Ragout with Baby Vegetables

Spring Ragout with Baby Vegetables

This is one of those super-simple dishes where the quality of the ingredients—really fresh, perfectly seasonal vegetables—is what makes it. In Odesa, people start preparing the stew from around the beginning of May, as soon as the new young vegetables appear in the markets. The delicacy of the vegetables is enhanced by the butter and sour cream. Victoria has shared her family's recipe, which came from her grandmother Jacqueline who was born in Odesa. Her grandmother's name doesn't sound very Ukrainian, but that's because her husband, Victoria's granddad, gave his wife a French nickname to praise her elegance and beauty. When Victoria was a child, she loved watching her granny making this dish for her in her tiny cozy kitchen.

2 lb (1 kg) baby new potatoes

14 oz (400 g) young carrots

21 oz (600 g) mini zucchini

18 oz (500 g) young cabbage (preferably sweetheart cabbage)

4 jumbo spring onions

3 stems young fresh green garlic

1¾ oz (50 g) fresh flat-leaf parsley

1¾ oz (50 g) fresh dill

3½ oz (100 g) butter

12¼ oz (350 g) small fresh English peas

9 oz (250 g) sour cream

Sea salt

SERVES 6–8

Peel the potatoes. Peel and cut the carrots into rounds. Halve the zucchini lengthwise and cut into pieces. Shred the cabbage. Slice the onions into half-rings. Separate the cloves from the young garlic and finely chop. Chop the parsley and dill.

Have a large saucepan ready for the stew. Melt the butter in a large frying pan over medium heat. Lightly sauté the vegetables one by one, then transfer each sautéed vegetable into the saucepan as you go: start with the potatoes, then the carrots, zucchini, cabbage, onions, and garlic. Do not add water; the young vegetables will release enough liquid while cooking.

Cover the saucepan with a lid and let the vegetables simmer for 10 minutes. Then add the peas, parsley, dill, sour cream, and salt to taste. Stir gently and simmer for 5 to 10 minutes, or until the vegetables are tender. Carefully mix the stew and serve hot.

Roasted Eggplant "Caviar"

The "holy dish" of Odesa's cooking is eggplant caviar. Vegetable caviars appear all over Eastern Europe and are eternally popular. This version by Elena and her father uses roasted or grilled vegetables, which give the finished dish an extra depth and smokiness. I met Elena many years ago when she came to my cooking school, and we hit it off straightaway. Our debates about the most authentic recipes in Odesa became legendary. There are so many recipes for eggplant caviar in Odesa, but I really like this one, which Elena's father perfected to a T.

3 eggplants

4 yellow bell peppers

3 tomatoes

1 red onion

2½ tablespoons sunflower oil

1 teaspoon cider vinegar

4 large cloves garlic, crushed

A handful of fresh flat-leaf parsley, chopped

Sea salt

Rye bread

SERVES 10

Preheat the oven to 450°F (230°C). Line a large baking sheet with aluminum foil. Pierce each eggplant on both sides with a fork.

Arrange the eggplants, bell peppers, and tomatoes in a single layer on the prepared baking sheet. Roast, turning the vegetables occasionally, for 30 to 40 minutes, or until they are very soft and the skins are slightly charred. Transfer the peppers to a bowl, cover with plastic wrap, and let steam so the skins will loosen. Let the eggplants and tomatoes cool on the baking sheet.

Peel the onion and cut it into small cubes. When the vegetables are cool enough to handle but are still warm, using a paring knife, peel off and discard the skins. Remove the seeds from the peppers. Finely chop the eggplants and tomatoes. Cut the peppers into small cubes. Mix the vegetables together in a large bowl. Add the sunflower oil, vinegar, garlic, and parsley, season with salt, and mix everything well. Serve at room temperature or chilled on top of rye bread.

NOTE

You can also use a barbecue grill to roast the vegetables and add more flavor (like Odesan people usually do during summer season in their dachas*). We also have a version of eggplant caviar, or paste, that is called "raw" in Odesa. In that version, only the eggplants are roasted, and parsley and bell peppers are not added, but ground black pepper and plenty of garlic are a must, and you absolutely need very ripe and meaty tomatoes.*

Roasted Eggplant "Caviar"

Zucchini "Caviar"

Zucchini "Caviar"

This is a story of a beautiful exchange. Lena travels the world, spending a lot of time in her beloved Africa where she works with local communities, then brings many exotic ingredients back to her Odesa home. Katenka is a chef in Lena's house and has become more like a family member. An amazing, intuitive cook who knows Odesan food well, Katenka has also been happy to learn how to use new ingredients from Lena. Katenka in turn has taught Lena how to make the food of their homeland. Both are keen on light and vibrant dishes.

This "caviar" recipe is one such dish. Made with zucchini, it is a delicate and simple recipe. You can eat it hot or chilled straight from the fridge with a slice of white sourdough bread. Thank you, Katenka, for sharing with us a few "nuances" of this summer recipe. Adding carrots isn't common but lends the dish a whole new level of color and sweetness. The importance of only lightly frying the vegetables is another key tip. But the main secret is using fresh vegetables in season.

2 onions

2 large zucchini

3 tomatoes

1 large carrot

2 small cloves garlic

Sunflower oil for frying

Sea salt and freshly ground pepper

A handful of fresh flat-leaf parsley, chopped

A handful of fresh dill, chopped

SERVES 10–12

Peel and dice the onions. Cut the zucchini and tomatoes into small cubes. Peel and grate the carrot. Peel and finely chop the garlic.

Heat sunflower oil in a nonstick or heavy-bottomed saucepan over medium heat. Fry the onions until golden brown. Add the zucchini, season with salt, and stir well. Cover with a lid and cook on low heat for 5 to 7 minutes. Add the carrot, cover, and cook for 5 minutes. Add the tomatoes and garlic, and season with salt and pepper, then stir and cook uncovered for 7 to 10 minutes. Garnish with the parsley and dill. Serve as an appetizer, hot or cold.

NOTE

Depending on the season, you can use jumbo spring onions and stems of young fresh green garlic for this dish, like we usually do in Odesa. You will need 2 jumbo spring onions and 1 stem green garlic. We serve zucchini paste as a separate dish or on slices of fresh rye or white bread.

Colorful Tomato Salad

A tomato salad is a must at most meals during the summer in Odesa, often made with several varieties, like in this recipe. The king of Odesan tomatoes is the Mikado (see page 16), a rare variety with a short season. A single tomato can weigh 21 to 25 oz (600 to 700 g) and could serve as an entire meal. The Odesan terroir, flanked by the steppe and the sea, gives this tomato a sweet-salty flavor and an incredible aroma.

We made this salad with Anna, the owner of a deli specializing in Italian products, and her father, who knows a lot about tomatoes. Their family comes from a mixed Bulgarian-Ukrainian origin. "Tomatoes with bread and cheese is what villagers in Bessarabia typically have for breakfast," Anna's dad explains. For this salad, it's important to use heirloom tomatoes—such as Bull's Heart, yellow, cherry, Margold, Green Zebra, and plum tomatoes—of different colors and sizes for a range of flavors and visual appeal.

1 large red onion

3 shallots

Juice of ½ lemon

Sea salt and freshly ground pepper

Unrefined sunflower oil as needed

2 lb (1 kg) multicolored heirloom tomatoes of different sizes

Sourdough white bread

SERVES 4–6

Peel and thinly slice the onion and shallots and transfer to a large bowl. Drizzle with the lemon juice, season with salt and pepper, and lightly drizzle with sunflower oil. Let stand for about 10 minutes to marinate.

Cut the tomatoes into randomly-size pieces (small tomatoes can be halved), then mix the tomatoes and any juices they have released with the marinated onion and shallots. Add more sunflower oil and season with salt to taste. Serve immediately with bread.

Colorful Tomato Salad

Roasted Peppers with Two Dressings

Roasted Peppers with Two Dressings

Nothing sums up the spirit of an Odesan summer quite like the aroma of frying or roasting peppers wafting from open windows. Families have countless recipes involving peppers and here's one from Alla: roasted and peeled peppers dressed with a choice of two contrasting sauces. Alla comes from a Jewish family that embraces what we like to call a true cult of food. All the women in her family were excellent cooks, in particular her grandmother Polya, who was known throughout the entire neighborhood. Alla herself is a larger-than-life character who has inherited Polya's love of food. Now she owns a restaurant (and a beach!) in the city where you can sample both these dishes. Choose one of the two marinades, sweet or savory.

3¼ lb (1.5 kg) bell peppers (about 12 peppers)

SWEET MARINADE

2 tablespoons unrefined sunflower oil

About 6 tablespoons (3 fl oz/100 ml) liquid from the cooked peppers

1 teaspoon honey

1 teaspoon fresh lemon juice

6 cloves garlic, peeled and minced

Sea salt and freshly ground pepper

SAVORY MARINADE

2 tablespoons unrefined sunflower oil

About 6 tablespoons (3 fl oz/100 ml) liquid from the cooked peppers

1 tablespoon cider vinegar

6 cloves garlic, peeled and minced

Sea salt and freshly ground pepper

SERVES 6

Preheat the oven to 350°F (180°C).

Put the bell peppers on a baking sheet and roast for 30 to 40 minutes, depending on the variety.

Place the hot roasted peppers in a sealed plastic bag and let stand for 20 minutes. Then peel off the skins and remove the stems and seeds. Collect the liquid from the peppers and strain it through a fine-mesh sieve if necessary to remove any seeds.

For the sweet marinade, in a bowl, stir together the sunflower oil, reserved liquid from the cooked peppers, honey, lemon juice, garlic, 1 teaspoon salt, and ½ teaspoon pepper until well combined.

For the savory marinade, in a bowl, stir together the sunflower oil, reserved liquid from the cooked peppers, vinegar, garlic, 1 teaspoon salt, and ½ teaspoon pepper until well combined.

The peppers can be served either hot or cold.

For hot peppers: Arrange the warm peppers on a serving dish, pour the marinade over them, and let stand for 10 to 15 minutes before serving.

For cold peppers: Place the warm peppers in a glass container, pour the marinade over them, cover, and refrigerate. They can be refrigerated for up to 3 weeks.

NOTE
For the savory version, you can replace the liquid from the cooked peppers with 3½ oz (100 g) grated ripe tomato.

Flecked Bean Tzimmes

Odesan cuisine is all about the important nuances—small but very important details about how to source, cook, and even slice an ingredient, like in this recipe. It's crucial to slice the onions very evenly into fine rings, about ¼ inch (5 mm) thick. And then you must fry them really slowly in plenty of good sunflower oil so they turn nicely browned and caramelized. I got this advice on how to fry the onions from Oleg, who said he was sad that many people no longer make this dish; they complained it was too much hassle. It's such a shame, as I think this is one of the most surprising recipes in this book and is easy enough to prepare. Humble beans cooked long and slow are turned into a kind of hummus, then topped with a gorgeous topping of rich, fried onions.

12½ oz (350 g) dried borlotti beans

9 large onions

Sunflower oil for frying and drizzling

1 oz (30 g) superfine (caster) sugar

Sea salt and freshly ground pepper

SERVES 10

Place the beans in a saucepan, cover with cold water, and let them soak overnight. In the morning, place the saucepan over high heat and bring to a boil, then reduce the heat to medium and simmer the beans for 3 hours, or until they are soft.

While the beans are cooking, peel and slice the onions into fine rings (the shape is important). Heat the sunflower oil in a large frying pan over medium heat. Add the onions and fry for about 30 minutes, or until they caramelize and turn a rich, deep brown. Set aside 2 tablespoons of the fried onions for garnish.

Add the remaining fried onions while they are still warm, along with their frying oil, to the hot beans and mix thoroughly. Add the sugar and season with salt and pepper.

Pass the bean mixture twice through a meat grinder. Transfer to a serving plate, drizzle with sunflower oil, and garnish with the reserved fried onions.

NOTE

You can use a stick blender as well but for the authentic texture, it's better to use a meat grinder (which is an Odesan maman*'s favorite gadget). With a stick blender, pulse the beans and onions into a thick puree; it doesn't need to be completely smooth.*

Flecked Bean Tzimmes

Eggplant in Sour Cream "Like Mushrooms"

Eggplant in Sour Cream "Like Mushrooms"

Katerina is what we call "a cook from God," meaning she feels food and cooking really well, despite never being professionally trained. She was often invited to cater at events, especially weddings. Katerina's parents live in a village close to Odesa, where she goes as much as she can, not the least to use the *pich*, a proper old Slavic masonry oven, for baking (her Easter paska buns are legendary). For the last few years, Katerina has been working as a cook for a family. This is a well-off household that appreciates really good food but lacks the time to make it. This setup is not uncommon in the city with a "cult of food," where people would choose home-cooked meals rather than buying premade dishes, no matter how fancy. Oh, and this dish is called "like mushrooms" because the final result looks and even tastes like another well-known mushroom dish!

21 oz (600 g) eggplants

Sea salt and freshly ground pepper

10½ oz (300 g) onions

4½ tablespoons (2¼ fl oz/70 ml) sunflower oil, plus more if needed

1¾ oz (50 g) sour cream

SERVES 4–6

Peel the eggplants and cut them into large cubes. Place the eggplant cubes on a paper towel and add a few pinches of salt; let stand for 15 minutes. Peel and cut the onions into large cubes.

Heat the sunflower oil in 2 large frying pans over medium heat. Sauté the eggplants and onions in separate pans, stirring constantly, until golden brown. Add a little more oil while frying the eggplants if the pan starts to look a bit dry. Toss the fried eggplants and onions into a colander to drain off the oil.

In one of the frying pans over medium-low heat, sauté the fried eggplants, onions, and sour cream together. Season with salt and pepper to taste. Serve as an appetizer, hot or cold.

Korean-ish Carrots from Odesa

This dish is a prime example of the unique mix of industry and cosmopolitan influences that make up Odesa. In my family these carrots have to be on the table for the most important holiday of the year—New Year's Eve. We even have a special plate with five sections, which we use just for this salad, and serve it alongside four other "Korean" appetizers.

First of all, I should say that this dish doesn't actually exist in Korea itself. The recipe comes from the so-called Koryo-saram people—ethnic Koreans living in the post-Soviet space. The so-called Korean carrots are known to everyone from the Soviet Union, but not many people know that its popularity can be traced back to Odesa and the Karyosaram family of Kapitalina VasilyevNa Tsoi. In the challenging 1980s, Kapitalina's family started to sell carrots made with Korean spices at the Privoz Market. This salad was selling so quickly that they had to expand at a crazy rate, selling at other markets and eventually even hiring people. The recipe couldn't be kept a total secret, of course, and soon versions of these carrots could be seen for sale across the city, Ukraine, and farther afield. At first, Kapitalina's family didn't know what to do, as they began losing control of their mini empire. But they soon regrouped and got to work creating a small but well-run business with their own uniform, branding, and equipment.

This particular adaptation of the recipe comes from Oksana, a close friend of Kapitalina's family. She now lives in the United States and spreads the popularity of these Korean carrots among Americans.

2 lb (1 kg) carrots

3 cloves garlic

Sea salt

1 teaspoon superfine (caster) sugar

1 tablespoon ground coriander

1 tablespoon sunflower oil

½ tablespoon rice vinegar

MAKES ENOUGH FOR A 1-QUART (34-FL OZ/1-L) JAR

Peel the carrots and grate them along their entire length into a large bowl. Press the garlic through a garlic press and set aside (do not add it to the bowl yet).

Add 1 tablespoon salt to the carrots and shake them about in the bowl. Do not mash the carrots with your hands or use spoons or spatulas to mix the ingredients. Add the sugar and shake again. Add the coriander and shake. Add the garlic and shake. Finally, add the sunflower oil and vinegar. The carrot salad can be served immediately or stored in the fridge in a 1-quart (34-fl oz/1-l) sterilized jar for up to 3 weeks.

NOTE

Oksana adapted the recipe to suit her taste and changed coriander to ground cumin, and I really like both versions. Also, she noted that it is important not to mash the carrots as this will help preserve their crunch and shape. If you are a fan of spicy food, you can add ½ teaspoon cayenne pepper or more to taste.

Korean-ish Carrots from Odesa

Borsch and More

SOUPS AND BROTHS

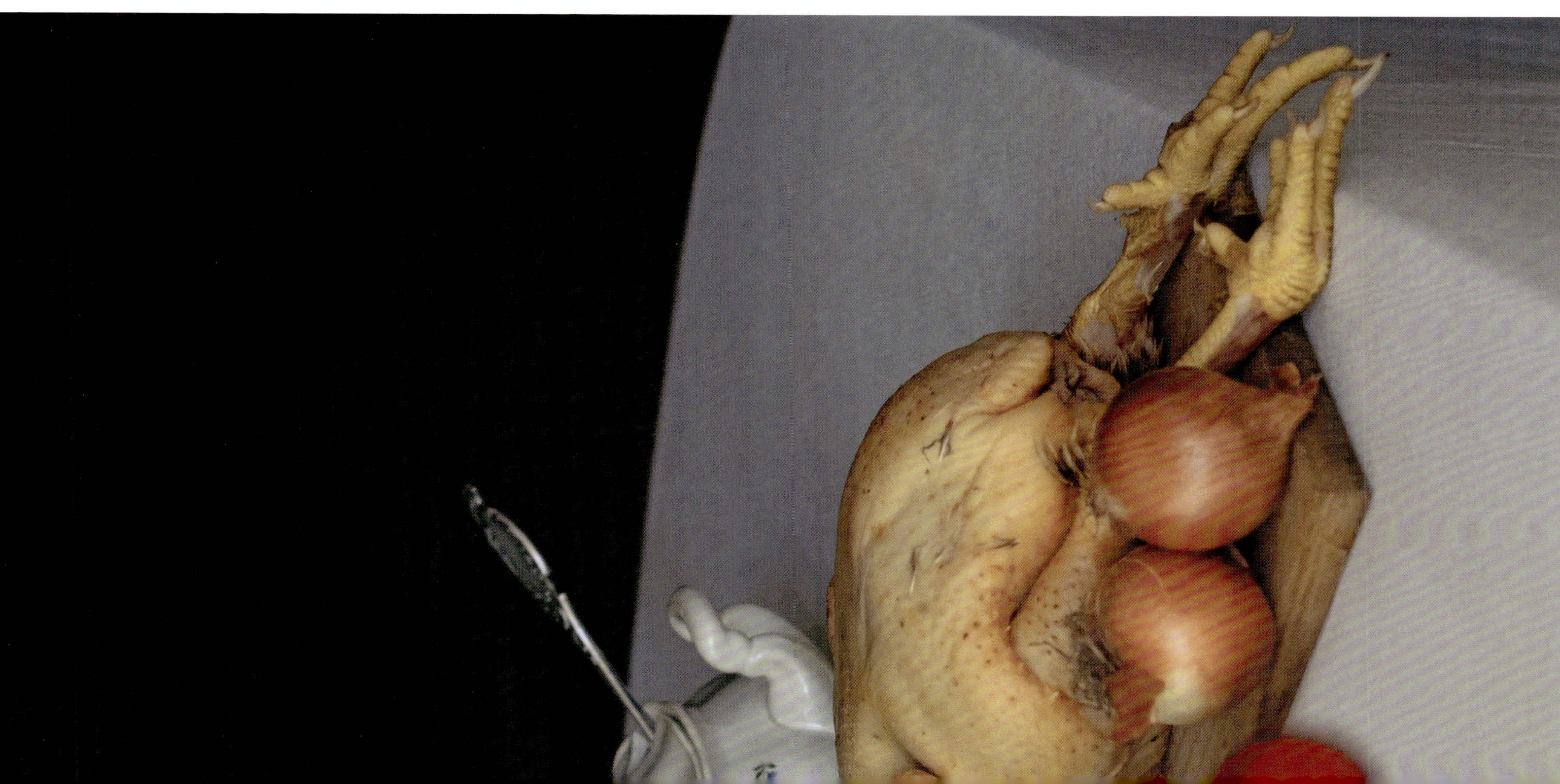

Summer Green Borsch

Summer Green Borsch

There is something of a sorcerer about this dish—a big cauldron bubbling on the stove with lots of different herbs and a mighty beef bone! The soup is a beautiful example of how Ukrainian food can be light, absolutely delicious, and so good for you. I was taught how to make this borsch by Ivan, a chef who has worked in some of the best restaurants in Odesa. He explained that you can add other herbs to the mix here (nettles and wild garlic are particularly good if you can get ahold of them).

I'm proud to say that this Ukrainian recipe will also appear in the upcoming cookbook by Natasha MacAller, aka the Dancing Chef. Natasha has been a very important person to me while I was working on my book, becoming a mentor and a big supporter and seeing the potential of my vision for a book on Odesa early on, when I lacked confidence. Her belief in me gave me so much strength. When she asked me to contribute a recipe for her book, something from Ukraine with healing properties, I knew immediately that this borsch would be the perfect fit.

1 carrot

2 onions, divided

About 3½ tablespoons sunflower oil, divided

2 lb (1 kg) beef shank with bone

About 3 quarts (102 fl oz/3 l) plus 1 tablespoon cold water, divided

2 bay leaves

1 teaspoon allspice

Sea salt

10½ oz (300 g) potatoes

3½ oz (100 g) long-grain white rice

3 eggs

10½ oz (300 g) spinach

5¼ oz (150 g) sorrel

3½ oz (100 g) fresh flat-leaf parsley

3½ oz (100 g) fresh dill

1¾ oz (50 g) green onions

3 or 4 peppercorns

7 oz (200 g) sour cream

SERVES 8–10

To make the stock, peel and roughly chop the carrot and 1 of the onions. Heat 2 tablespoons of the sunflower oil in a large stockpot over medium heat. Add the carrot and onion and fry for 3 minutes. Add the beef, the cold water, the bay leaves, and allspice and season with salt. Bring to a boil, skimming any white residue off the top. Reduce the heat to low and simmer for 40 minutes. Transfer the beef to a bowl and set aside. Strain the stock through a fine-mesh sieve and discard the carrot, onion, and bay leaves.

Peel and cut the potatoes into cubes and add to the stock. Set the pot over medium-high heat and simmer for 5 minutes, then add the rice and simmer for 15 minutes, or until the potatoes and rice are tender.

Peel and finely chop the remaining onion. Heat the remaining 1½ tablespoons sunflower oil in a frying pan over medium heat, add the onion, and fry until golden brown. Remove from the heat. Cut the beef into large cubes. Set aside.

In a small bowl, beat the eggs with the 1 tablespoon water until smooth. Finely chop the spinach, sorrel, parsley, dill, and green onions. While stirring the borsch slowly, pour in the egg mixture, then remove from the heat. Add the beef, fried onion, spinach, sorrel, parsley, dill, green onions, and peppercorns and season with salt. Remove from the heat. Cover the pot with a lid and let the borsch rest for 5 minutes. Ladle into soup bowls, top with a spoonful of sour cream, and serve.

Fontansky Borsch with Fried Gobies

Most people now know that borsch is a beet-based soup, made with or without meat. This recipe is a lesser-known but equally delicious borsch prepared with freshly caught fish from the Black Sea. Unlike traditional borsch, the soup is best eaten on the day it's made, either at room temperature or chilled during the summer. It is served without sour cream, which you would normally have with borsch. During Lent, the period before Easter when Orthodox Christians are supposed to abstain from eating fish and meat, you omit the fish but add the beet greens instead. They have a distinctly different flavor than the beets themselves—stringent and more iron-y, as if spinach had a beet cousin. Using the whole vegetable is also very Odesan—it avoids food waste and is really good for you.

1 white onion

1 large carrot

2 young beets, greens trimmed and reserved

6 tomatoes

2 potatoes

A handful of fresh flat-leaf parsley

A handful of fresh dill

3 spring onions

½ green cabbage

About 6 tablespoons (3 fl oz/100 ml) sunflower oil, divided

1 teaspoon superfine (caster) sugar

Juice of ½ lemon

2 bay leaves

Peppercorns

Sea salt

6–8 fried gobies (see page 128)

SERVES 4–6

Peel and dice the white onion. Peel the carrot and beets and cut into thin strips. Cut the tomatoes in half and grate them into a bowl. Peel and dice the potatoes. Finely chop the parsley, dill, and spring onions. Finely shred the cabbage and beet greens.

Heat 3 tablespoons of the sunflower oil in a large frying pan over medium heat. Add the white onion and carrot and lightly sauté. At the same time, heat the remaining 3 tablespoons sunflower oil in another large frying pan over medium heat. Add the beets and fry, then add the tomatoes, sugar, and lemon juice and fry.

Pour about 3 quarts (102 fl oz/3 l) water into a large saucepan and bring to a boil over medium-high heat. Add the potatoes, bay leaves, a few peppercorns, the sautéed white onion and carrot, parsley, dill, and spring onions. Simmer for 5 minutes, then add the cabbage and beet greens. Simmer for 5 minutes, then add the fried beets and tomatoes. Season with salt and simmer for 5 minutes. Carefully add the fried gobies to the pan. Remove from the heat and let the borsch stand for a while to infuse the flavors.

Fontansky Borsch with Fried Gobies

Winter Soup Rozsolnyk

Winter Soup Rozsolnyk

This soup is made in different parts of Eastern Europe in a variety of ways, but the single ingredient that unites them all is salted cucumbers. *Rozsol* means that squint-your-eyes, sour-and-sweet brine you get when salting cucumbers, so look for this type of gherkin in Polish and other Eastern European shops. The recipe was passed on to me by Sasha Sokalskaya, an Odesan female chef who rose to fame thanks to her love of gutsy, south Ukrainian flavors. When she told her mum she was working on her rozsolnyk recipe for this book, she got a text message back from her mum at 3 a.m. that said, "Must peel cucumbers." Sasha quickly texted back to ask why. The reply immediately came back, "I love it when the cucumbers melt in your mouth. When you peel them, they are as soft as a cloud." And so we are following her advice. Let them be peeled.

3½ oz (100 g) pearl barley

1¼ cups (10 fl oz/300 ml) cold water, plus more for rinsing

2 small onions

1 large carrot

3 large cloves garlic, divided

10½ oz (300 g) red potatoes

18 oz (500 g) kosher dill pickles

18 oz (500 g) chicken legs, preferably corn-fed and organi

About 3½ tablespoons sunflower oil, divided

1 teaspoon allspice

3 bay leaves

About 2 quarts (68 fl oz/2 l) hot water

Sea salt

A handful of chopped fresh dill

SERVES 4–6

Rinse the barley several times with cold water and drain. Pour the 1¼ cups cold water into a saucepan, add the barley, and bring to a boil over high heat. Reduce the heat to medium and simmer the barley for about 30 minutes, or until tender. Drain off any excess water, then rinse the barley well to remove any excess starch that could darken the soup. Set aside.

Peel the onions, carrot, and garlic. Cut the onions and carrot into very small cubes. Make a puree from 1 garlic clove and smash the remaining cloves with the side of a knife. Peel and dice the potatoes. Dice the pickles. Cut each chicken leg into 2 parts.

Heat 2 tablespoons of the sunflower oil in a large stockpot over low heat. Add the smashed garlic, allspice, bay leaves, and chicken legs and cook to gently caramelize the chicken. When the chicken skin starts to brown, add the hot water to the pot and let it simmer gently.

Meanwhile, heat the remaining 1½ tablespoons sunflower oil in a large frying pan. Add the onions, carrot, and garlic puree and sauté over very low heat until soft; you want to avoid browning.

When the chicken is tender, add the potatoes and the sautéed vegetables to the soup and simmer for 3 minutes. Then add the cooked barley and pickles and season with salt. Cover the pot with a lid and simmer for 7 to 10 minutes, or until the chicken is cooked through and all the ingredients are tender. Add the dill just before serving.

Black Sea Sprat Soup

Since he was a little boy, Ruslan would go to the New Market in Odesa with his grandmother and mother, who would teach him the culture of market shopping: how to choose (and keep) your vendors, what is best to buy on which days, how to haggle, and who has the freshest fish. Looking for inexpensive but really good-quality ingredients has always been important to Odesans. So even in the last twenty years, when most things have become available in supermarkets, the tradition of shopping at food markets, for food, but also as an integral part of the cultural code, has remained. This fish soup made with local sprats was one of the first dishes to become a Ruslan family tradition—quick, easy, and fun. Ruslan's wife, Lena, learned this recipe soon after the couple got married and continued making it ever since. Now the whole family, including their kids, go to the market in search of the best ingredients, to haggle, to banter, and to learn how to prepare the soup at home.

2 lb (1 kg) Black Sea sprats or fresh anchovies

3 young carrots

4 potatoes

3 tomatoes

1 red bell pepper

3½ oz (100 g) celery root

1 parsley root

1 onion, unpeeled

2 cloves garlic, peeled

2 bay leaves

5 peppercorns

6½ cups (52 fl oz/1.5 l) cold water

Sea salt

A handful of fresh flat-leaf parsley, finely chopped

A handful of fresh dill, finely chopped

SERVES 4–6

Fillet the fish by removing the heads and backbones, leaving the fillets free of any bones. Peel and slice the carrots into rounds. Peel and cut the potatoes into 4 to 6 pieces, rinsing them under cold water to remove the starch. Cut the tomatoes into quarters. Remove the seeds from the bell pepper and dice it.

Place the celery root, parsley root, carrots, onion, garlic, bay leaves, and peppercorns in a large stockpot and pour in the cold water. Bring to a boil over medium heat and season with salt. Remove the celery root and parsley root and discard. Add the potatoes, tomatoes, and bell pepper to the pot. Simmer over low heat for about 10 minutes, or until the potatoes are tender. Remove the onion and discard, then add the fish. Bring the soup to a boil over medium-high heat, then immediately remove from the heat. Cover the pot with a lid and let the soup rest for at least 30 minutes to allow the flavors to develop.

Since this is a summer soup, it is best served warm, not piping hot. Garnish with the parsley and dill just before serving.

Black Sea Sprat Soup

Cold Kefir Summer Soup

Cold Kefir Summer Soup

"Odesa for me is my favorite place in the world. And the best place to eat," Alexander Mardan told me. A proud Odesan and a bit of a legend in the city, he is a playwright whose plays have been staged all around Ukraine and in many other countries. Alexander recounts how in Greece, a place would earn the title of a "city" once a theater was built there. Well, in Odesa there are enough theaters for at least ten cities! And almost all of them had Mardan's plays performed in them. Cold soups are a very important family of recipes in Ukraine since summers are very hot and you can put together a soup like this quickly in the morning so that it chills in the fridge until you're ready to eat in the afternoon or evening.

2 small white onions, divided

10½ oz (300 g) veal fillet

4 bay leaves, divided

8 peppercorns, divided

Sea salt

10½ oz (300 g) boneless, skinless chicken breasts

3 eggs

6 small cucumbers

12¼ oz (350 g) radishes

5 cups (40 fl oz/1.2 l) cold kefir

2½ cups (20 fl oz/600 ml) cold sparkling natural mineral water

2 teaspoons mustard

½ teaspoon fresh lemon juice

⅓ bunch fresh flat-leaf parsley

⅓ bunch fresh dill

4 spring onions

SERVES 6–8

Peel the onions. Bring a saucepan of tap water to a boil over high heat. There should be enough water to cover the veal. Add the veal, 1 of the white onions, 2 of the bay leaves, and 4 of the peppercorns. Season with salt and simmer for 1 hour, or until the veal is tender. Let the meat cool in the broth so it stays juicy.

Fill another large saucepan with tap water and bring it to a boil over high heat. There should be enough water to cover the chicken. Add the chicken and the remaining white onion, 2 bay leaves, and 4 peppercorns. Season with salt and simmer for 30 minutes, or until the chicken is cooked through. Let the meat cool in the broth so it stays juicy.

Put the eggs into a saucepan of cold water and bring to a boil over high heat. As soon as the water comes to a rolling boil, reduce heat to low, cook the eggs for 10 minutes, then plunge them into cold water before peeling off the shells. Dice the eggs, cucumbers, radishes, veal, and chicken into small cubes. Place each ingredient in a separate bowl without mixing them.

In a large bowl, combine the kefir and sparkling water. Add the mustard and lemon juice, season with salt, and stir well. Finely chop the parsley, dill, and spring onions. Add them to the kefir mixture and stir.

Just before serving, assemble the dish directly into soup bowls. Divide the eggs, cucumbers, radishes, veal, and chicken among the bowls. Pour a good helping of the well-chilled kefir mixture on top and serve.

NOTE

If you're not serving the soup immediately, refrigerate the kefir and herb mixture until ready to use. You can swap in ayran (a yogurt drink) for the kefir; you will need 6½ cups (52 fl oz/1.5 l) ayran and only 1¼ cups (10 fl oz/300 ml) mineral water.

Odesan "French" Soup

This is a very light and vibrant spring soup made from young vegetables just in season. "So what makes this soup French?" I asked Regina, an Odesan who now lives in Berlin and has a long lineage of ancestors who were born in Odesa. She explained that during Soviet times, calling someone French was a coded way of saying they were Jewish. It was more acceptable, at a time when being Jewish was at best a barrier against advancing in your career and at worst, downright dangerous. Regina learned this recipe when she grew up in a communal flat in Odesa where most residents, including her own family, were described as French.

VEGETABLE STOCK

1 parsley root

1 parsnip

¼ celery root

1 carrot

2 small onions

6 peppercorns

1 bay leaf

About 2½ quarts (85 fl oz/2.5 l) cold water

SOUP

2 large potatoes

½ cauliflower, trimmed

1 large carrot

3 tablespoons long-grain white rice

Sea salt

1¾ oz (50 g) butter

5¼ oz (150 g) fresh English peas

A handful of fresh flat-leaf parsley, chopped

A handful of fresh dill, chopped

Sour cream

SERVES 6–8

To make the stock, peel the parsley root, parsnip, and celery root. Leave the carrot and onions unpeeled. Place the parsley root, parsnip, celery root, carrot, onions, celery, peppercorns, and bay leaf in a large stockpot and pour in the cold water. Bring to a boil over high heat, then reduce the heat and simmer for 25 minutes. Discard the vegetables from the stock.

To make the soup, peel and dice the potatoes. Cut the cauliflower into florets. Scrub and grate the carrot. Add the potatoes, cauliflower, and rice to the pot with the stock and season with salt. In a frying pan over medium heat, melt the butter. Add the carrot and sauté briefly, then add to the soup along with the peas. Simmer the soup over medium-low heat for 10 to 15 minutes, or until the vegetables are tender, adding the parsley and dill during the last 2 minutes of cooking. Serve topped with a spoonful of sour cream.

Odesan "French" Soup

вулиця
КІННА
12

A Very Bright Chicken Borsch

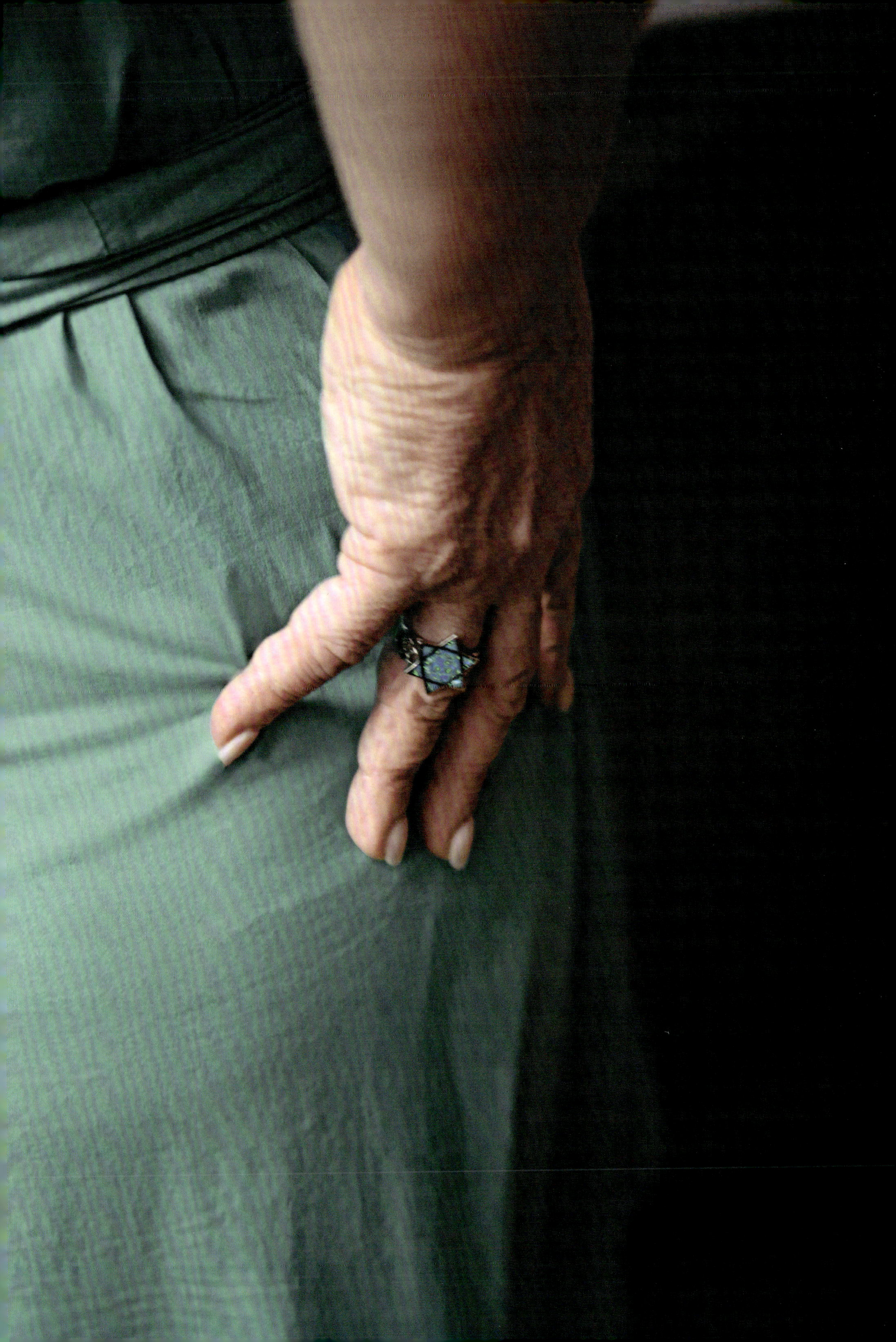

A Very Bright Chicken Borsch

"The Odesan borsch needs to be bright!" insists Margarita, an exuberant, stylishly dressed woman who is a bit of a celebrity in the city. She is a psychologist and lecturer who's been married for decades to Boris Bukhman, a photographer. They are a wonderful example of a truly Odesan couple: dynamic, intelligent, and charismatic, who do lots of good in the world and love to cook and eat well.

Several steps in the recipe are designed to retain the vibrant red color of the soup until the end, such as adding the beets late in the cooking process, along with the grated tomatoes. This dish is a Jewish version of the Ukrainian beet soup—the latter is normally made with beef, duck, or vegetarian, while Jewish borsch is prepared with a *domashnyaya*, a "home-reared" chicken. Margarita insists that you must include the chicken feet in the broth—first "manicured," she jokes—as the bones will give even more flavor to the dish.

Margarita explains how you can make this soup in stages: cook the broth, beets, and the rest of the vegetables separately in advance and then "marry" everything half an hour before sitting down to dinner. Long live borsch!

1 whole chicken, about 2¾ lb (1.2 kg) (preferably corn-fed and organic)

2 beets

2 potatoes

½ cabbage

¼ celery root

1 parsley root

2 carrots

1 large onion

About 6 tablespoons (3 fl oz/100 ml) sunflower oil

4 tomatoes

Place the chicken in a 5¼-quart (5-l) pot, cover with cold water, and bring to a boil over medium-high heat. Skim off any foam, reduce the heat to low, and cover with a lid. Simmer for at least 30 minutes, or until the chicken is tender. Transfer the chicken from the broth to a large bowl, let it cool, and separate the meat from the bones. Chop the meat into small pieces. Keep the broth warm over very low heat.

Meanwhile, carefully scrub the beets to remove any dirt. Place in a small saucepan, cover with water, and bring to a boil over high heat. Reduce the heat and simmer for 20 minutes. Let the beets cool, then peel. Dice 1 beet and grate the other beet; this will give the soup a variety of textures and enhance the vibrant color.

Cut the potatoes into cubes. Shred the cabbage into thin strips. Place the potatoes and cabbage in a medium saucepan, add a small amount of water, and bring to a boil over high heat. Cover with a lid, reduce the heat, and simmer for about 15 minutes. Remove from the heat and reserve the cooking liquid.

Peel and dice the celery root, parsley root, carrots, and onion. Heat the sunflower oil in a large frying pan over medium heat. Add the celery root, parsley root, and carrots and sauté, then add the onion and sauté until the onion is golden. Remove from the heat.

Cut the tomatoes in half and grate them into a bowl.

9 oz (250 g) canned butter beans, drained

A handful of fresh flat-leaf parsley, roughly chopped

A handful of fresh dill, roughly chopped

Sea salt

1 tablespoon superfine (caster) sugar

Peeled garlic cloves

Sourdough rye bread

5¼ oz (150 g) sour cream

SERVES 8–10

Return the chicken broth to a boil. Add the cooked potatoes and cabbage along with about 2¼ cups (17 fl oz/500 ml) of their cooking liquid. Add the butter beans, chicken, sautéed celery root mixture, and diced and grated beets. Simmer for 10 minutes.

Add the grated tomatoes to the soup. The acidity in the tomatoes helps the beets retain their color. Bring to a boil and simmer for 5 minutes, then add the parsley and dill. Season with salt and sugar to balance the acidity. Let the soup simmer for 5 minutes more, then reduce the heat and simmer gently for 3 minutes.

Serve the borsch with garlic cloves, rye bread, and a spoonful of sour cream.

NOTE

Margarita always used broth made from a chicken carcass as she is a very experienced home chef and cooks five dishes from one chicken. During the winter, when there are no good tomatoes in Odesa, she uses tomato paste for borsch instead. For this recipe you will need 2 tablespoons of good tomato paste.

Under the Sea

FISH AND SHELLFISH

Fried Black Sea Turbot

Fried Black Sea Turbot

Eduard, who shared this recipe, describes himself as a dreamer, a winemaker, and a businessman—in that order. The terroir in this part of Ukraine is particularly favorable for making great wines, thanks to the unique, richly fertile chernozem soil and the proximity to the sea. Eduard is among the new breed of winemakers who make small quantities of wine, combining ancient techniques with modern technology. He sells his wines directly to customers in his wine bar, using his fantastic sense of humor to help the process. Here's one example of his offbeat humor: While we were shooting photos for this recipe in Sauvignon, a suburban area in Odesa, it seemed like every house had some delicious aromas of cooking wafting our way. So Eduard immediately renamed the town Zhravignon—a play on the Ukrainian word *zhrat*, which means to eat hungrily.

6½–9 lb (3–4 kg) turbot or flounder

Sea salt

About ⅔ cup (5 fl oz/150 ml) sunflower oil

5¼ oz (150 g) all-purpose flour

SERVES 6

Using a sharp knife, trim off the fins along the back and belly of the fish. Remove the side and tail fins with pruning shears. Carefully insert a knife into the anal opening and make a semicircular incision along the back, then repeat on the belly, starting from the same point. The incision should follow the shape of the head and end where the spine meets it. Cut through the spine with a sharp knife, then use pruning shears to completely remove the head. Pull away the head along with the innards, then gently separate and discard the guts. The head can be frozen to use later in fish soup.

Rinse the belly cavity thoroughly under cold running water. Run a knife along the backbone to begin splitting the fish in half. Use pruning shears to finish cutting through the backbone. Slice each half into strips 1¼ to 1½ inches (3 to 4 cm) wide, adjusting the width depending on the thickness of the fish, then cut into individual portions with the shears.

Line a plate with paper towels. Rub the fish pieces with salt. Heat the sunflower oil in a large frying pan over medium heat. Put the flour on a plate. Dredge the fish in the flour, shaking off any excess, then place in the hot pan. Add the fish and fry until golden and crispy on both sides. If the pieces are large, turn them to fry on all four sides for even cooking. Transfer the fried fish to the paper towel–lined plate to absorb any excess oil. Serve immediately.

Pan-Fried Red Mullet

"Everyone who was born in Odesa knows how to fry fish, it's in our blood," an Odesan food guide named Yulia told me when I naively asked her who taught her to fry fish so well. When one grows up in a communal flat, like Yulia and so many other Odesans, where all the neighbors fry fish in the same large kitchen at the same time during that particular fish season, you learn how to cook fish by default—you have no other option! Freshness is really the most important factor for a really good piece of fish, so Yulia goes to Privoz Market early in the morning whenever she fancies some nice fish. Which happens a lot. The smell and sound of fish being fried is like Proust's madeleine memory for Odesans, something you never forget. Delicious, savory, sizzling.

2 lb (1 kg) small whole red mullet

Sea salt and freshly ground pepper

7 oz (200 g) coarse cornmeal

About 6 tablespoons (3½ fl oz/100 ml) sunflower oil, plus more as needed

SERVES 4–6

Rinse the fish under cold running water and pat dry with paper towels. Season with salt and pepper. Put the cornmeal in a bowl. Dust each fish on both sides with cornmeal, putting a little inside the body cavity; holding the fish by the tail, shake off any excess.

Line a plate with paper towels. Pour the sunflower oil into a large frying pan to a depth of ⅜ inch (1 cm) and heat over medium heat until hot. Working in batches as needed, fry the fish on each side for 3 to 5 minutes, or until golden brown. Add more oil to the pan as needed to keep it ⅜ inch (1 cm) deep. Transfer the fried fish to the paper towel–lined plate to absorb any excess oil. Serve immediately.

Pan-Fried Red Mullet

3
ПЕРОВ

From the Girl with the Goby Tattoo

From the Girl with the Goby Tattoo

Gobies are probably the most emblematic fish of this part of the Black Sea and of Odesa. They have a delicate white flesh with few bones and a skin that takes on a delicious umami flavor when fried in cornmeal. Natasha is from an Odesan family who moved to Berlin many years ago. But she never forgot the taste of Black Sea gobies, which her grandmother often fried for her during the summer holidays. When she grew up, she bought a boat, learned how to sail it, and began catching fish that were quite similar to gobies in the lakes near Berlin. Then she started to feed the fried fish to her local friends to great success. Natasha even got a beautiful tattoo that looks like a goby on her forearm, so Odesa is always with her, wherever she goes.

2 lb (1 kg) large fresh anchovies, bluegills, or Black Sea gobies (about 6–8 fish)

Sea salt

3½ oz (100 g) cornmeal

About 4½ tablespoons (2¼ fl oz/70 ml) sunflower oil

1 lemon

SERVES 4

Clean the fish, remove the gills, and rinse thoroughly under cold running water. Place the fish on a cutting board. Insert a sharp knife into the belly near the tail and carefully cut along the belly up to the head. Open up the fish and pull out all internal organs. Rinse the inside of the fish under cold water, removing any blood or leftover entrails. Pat dry with paper towels or drain in a fine-mesh sieve. Sprinkle the fish with salt and let stand for 5 minutes.

Put the cornmeal on a plate. Dredge each fish in the cornmeal, which will create a crispier crust.

Line a plate with paper towels. Heat the sunflower oil in a large frying pan over medium heat. Make sure the oil is well heated before adding the fish, as this prevents sticking. Add the fish and fry on both sides until golden brown. Transfer the fried fish to the paper towel–lined plate to absorb any excess oil. Cut the lemon into wedges and serve the fish with a squeeze of lemon juice.

Black Sea Mussels with Herbs

Mussels in Odesa are much more popular than, say, in the UK. Many of us grew up collecting mussels on beaches, then cleaning them and cooking the shellfish on makeshift grills by the sea. Washed down with cold white wine (Ukrainian, of course, chilled by burying the bottles deep in the sand on the shore!), this was our version of hip summers. This recipe comes from Anastasija, an Odesan restaurateur who was the first to dare to come to London, the food mecca of the world, to open a place dedicated solely to Odesan food. It was a restaurant in the center of the British capital, offering the food of her hometown but served in an elevated and elegant way. Anastasija and her team are now based in Tbilisi, Georgia, at a new restaurant that continues to carry the Odesan flag.

6½ lb (3 kg) fresh mussels
2 white onions
5 cloves garlic
15 spring onions
1 bunch fresh flat-leaf parsley
1 bunch fresh dill
About 2 tablespoons butter
1 bottle (750 ml) dry white wine, divided
Sea salt and freshly ground pepper
White bread

SERVES 6

Put the mussels in a large bowl filled with cold water and scrape off the barnacles with a knife, then remove the beards if needed. Peel and slice the white onions. Peel and finely chop the garlic. Trim and slice the spring onions. Roughly chop the parsley and dill.

Heat a large, deep frying pan over medium heat. Add the butter, about 3½ tablespoons water, the onions, and the garlic. Cover with a lid and simmer for 5 minutes. Then pour in half of the wine and 3¼ cups (26 fl oz/750 ml) water. Add the mussels, spring onions, parsley, and dill. Season with salt and pepper stir, cover, and simmer for 7 minutes. Pour in the remaining wine and about 1 cup (9 fl oz/250 ml) water. Stir well, cover, and continue simmering for 15 minutes, stirring every 5 minutes, until the shells have opened and the mussels have absorbed the flavors. Discard any unopened mussels. Serve the mussels in a deep bowl with white bread.

Black Sea Mussels with Herbs

Mussels with Salty Brynza Cheese

Mussels with Salty Brynza Cheese

Nadia Chebanov's restaurant on the beach, Kotelok, celebrates Odesan food from the sea. Kotelok means "a little cauldron," a pot used for cooking mussels, and this is the sole focus of Nadia's restaurant. The mussels from the Black Sea are as delicious as the ones you find in the Mediterranean. At Kotelok you can enjoy the freshest mussels prepared in a hundred different ways, including this one with brynza, a fresh salted cheese that is similar to feta.

I originally suggested this combination of ingredients when Nadia attended a master class at my cooking school many years ago. At the time restaurateurs were eager to use exotic ingredients in their dishes to attract customers, while I was promoting the importance of local food. I am so glad that Nadia and I were on the same wavelength. She put the dish on her menu and it has remained a favorite among her restaurant guests ever since.

6½ lb (3 kg) fresh mussels

3 shallots

3 bell peppers

6 cloves garlic

3 tomatoes

1 bunch fresh flat-leaf parsley

1 lemon

About 6 tablespoons (3 fl oz/100 ml) sunflower oil

About 1⅔ cups (13½ fl oz/400 ml) dry white wine

14 oz (400 g) salty sheep's milk cheese, such as Ukrainian brynza

SERVES 6

Put the mussels in a large bowl filled with cold water and scrape off the barnacles with a knife, then remove the beards if needed. Peel and slice the shallots. Slice the bell peppers. Peel and finely chop the garlic. Cut the tomatoes into small cubes. Finely chop the parsley. Cut the lemon into 6 wedges.

Heat the sunflower oil in a large frying pan over medium heat. Add the shallots and fry until transparent, then add the bell peppers and fry until tender.

Set a large pot over low heat. Transfer the shallots, bell peppers, and the oil remaining in the frying pan to the pot. Add the mussels and wine, cover with a lid, and simmer until the mussels begin to open. Then add the garlic and tomatoes and stir.

Crumble the cheese with your hands, add it to the pot, and stir. Cover and simmer until the cheese becomes soft (be careful, don't let it melt completely), then uncover the pot and add the parsley. Discard any unopened mussels. Serve the mussels in a deep bowl with the lemon wedges.

Vadim's Quintessential Forshmak

I met Vadim Chevganyuk in 2010 when I opened my culinary school. He was already an established chef in the city, known for his love of the authentic Odesan dishes that he was elevating to the level of fine dining. He had worked in Sophie Restaurant at the boutique Frederic Koklen Hotel, often demonstrating Odesan dishes to guests from overseas. Vadim became one of the most popular chefs in our school, thanks to his infectious personality and his passion for Odesan cuisine. There are many versions of forshmak, which is a quintessential Ashkenazi Jewish recipe. This dish might not sound that appetizing if you haven't grown up eating it. But it almost always wins you over once you've tried it. Vadim's pared-down version is probably the most traditional. Forshmak is a must-have dish on any Odesan feasting table.

10½ oz (300 g) salted herring fillets

9 oz (250 g) firm apples, such as Granny Smith

5¼ oz (150 g) cold butter

Sea salt and freshly ground pepper

Rye bread

SERVES 6

Coarsely grind the herring fillets in a food processor. Peel and core the apples. Coarsely grind the apples and butter in the meat mincer. Mix the herring, apples, and butter in a bowl. Season with salt and pepper. Chill the forshmak in the fridge for about 1 hour. Serve with rye bread.

NOTE
Traditionally we don't add any chile to forshmak, but if you want to spice it up, you can add some fresh red chile to taste.

Vadim's Quintessential Forshmak

В СВОЕМ ДВОРЕ!

Sofochka's Sprats in Batter

Sofochka's Sprats in Batter

The Black Sea is an important part of Odesan life. In fact, for Odesans the sea is a she (just like a boat is a she in English). The sea has no boundaries, so it's a daily reminder of the importance of freedom and a crucial part of the Odesan spirit. The sea provides people with access to the rest of the world, which is why Odesa has been such a strategic city for a long time. It is also a key source of food. Black Sea sprats are a popular food in the city and are used in many different recipes. Here Sofochka, the local *maman* and a great cook, makes sprat fritters. The size is very important. Each piece should consist of three sprats, no more and no less.

14 oz (400 g) fresh sprats
or fresh anchovies

1 small white onion

2 eggs

3 tablespoons all-purpose flour

Sea salt and
freshly ground pepper

About 6 tablespoons
(3 fl oz/100 ml) sunflower oil

SERVES 4

Rinse the fish under cold running water and pat dry with paper towels. Using kitchen scissors, cut off the head, then remove the guts from the belly. Open each fish and remove the backbone. Finely dice the onion.

In a bowl, whisk the eggs, then add the flour and season with salt and pepper. Mix until smooth. Stir in the onion. Add the fish to the batter and gently mix.

Heat the sunflower oil in a large frying pan over medium heat. Using a tablespoon, scoop portions of the mixture into the pan and fry for 3 to 5 minutes per side, or until fully cooked.

NOTE

If important guests are invited, our Odesan maman *Sofochka doesn't just toss the sprats into the batter. Instead, she carefully joins up three fish tail to tail, dips them into the batter, and lays them in the frying pan in the shape of an elegant fan. Sometimes, depending on her mood, she replaces the onion with finely chopped dill and parsley—after all, variety is the spice of life!*

Fish Roe Fritters

You can find different types of fish with roe at different times of the year at Odesan markets. The season starts in April with herring roe and ends the following March with bream eggs. In Odesa, fish is still mainly sold whole, so if you want a fish, you'll get the whole thing: complete with head, fins, and the roe. Nothing is wasted. This recipe was originally created out of necessity and maybe doesn't sound that appealing to the uninitiated, but I guarantee that you'll fall in love with these little fritters once you to taste them.

This recipe came from Garik's grandfather Pyotr Itskovich, who was a real patisserie master and founded the legendary café Skazka. Pyotr was once asked if the café got its name, which means fairy tale, because the cakes were just so magically delicious. No, he answered with a cheeky smile, the name came from the amazing profits the business generated. This was only possible, of course, because of the amazing cakes. Garik, who now lives in Tbilisi, opened his own bistro called Odesa, where many of his family's recipes are featured. Garik and this story reminded me of my own father: similarly handsome, full of energy, with a great respect for his roots and tongue-in-cheek sense of humor. Finding humor in all situations is an Odesan quality!

18 oz (500 g) pike perch or zander roe

1 egg

2 tablespoons all-purpose flour

¼ teaspoon baking soda

Sea salt and freshly ground pepper

¼ cup (2 fl oz/60 ml) sunflower oil

MAKES 10–12

Wash the roe with cold water. To clean the roe, place it on a cutting board. Using a knife, make small cuts in the membranes to open them up, being careful not to damage the roe. Use the knife to gently remove the membranes and films, then discard.

Mix the roe, egg, flour, baking soda, and season with salt and pepper in a bowl. The consistency should be like heavy cream.

Line a plate with paper towels. Heat the sunflower oil in a large frying pan over medium heat. When the oil is hot, add 1 tablespoon of the batter to make each fritter, being careful not to crowd the pan. Fry for 2 to 3 minutes on each side, or until crisp and golden brown. Transfer the fritters to the paper towel–lined plate to absorb any excess oil.

Fish Roe Fritters

Danube Herring with New Potatoes and Dill

Danube Herring with New Potatoes and Dill

Olga and Sergey, who work together as tour guide and chef, are both from Odesa. They told us that Vilkovo herring is especially renowned because of the tenderness of its fat. The fish swim from the Black Sea to the river for just a couple of months a year, developing a delicate, melt-in-your-mouth texture. Sergey suggests serving the herring with boiled new potatoes, dressed in a mixture of butter, unrefined sunflower oil, and dill. It's an example of the simple, highly seasonal food that Odesans crave whenever they're away from home for any length of time.

1 red onion

1 white onion

Boiling water for soaking

2 teaspoons sea salt

1 teaspoon caster sugar

2 tablespoon raw cider vinegar

5 tablespoons unrefined sunflower oil

2 lightly salted Danube whole herrings (or 4 herrings fillets)

2 pounds (1 kg) new potatoes

4¼ oz (120 g) spring onions, finely chopped

3½ oz (100 g) butter, thinly sliced

1¾ oz (50 g) fresh dill

SERVES 4–6

Slice both the red and white onions into thin rings, keeping them separate. Cover the sliced red onion with boiling water. Drain it, then season with 1 teaspoon of the salt, ½ teaspoon of the sugar, 1 tablespoon of the vinegar, and mix. Repeat with the white onion. Drizzle both sets of onions with a little sunflower oil and let them marinate in the fridge for 20 to 30 minutes.

Clean the herring. Cut off the head along with the pectoral fins. Use a knife or kitchen scissors to cut open the belly and remove the innards, then clean the belly thoroughly. Cut the herring into 1-cm-thick slices, including the backbone. Put it in the fridge.

Peel the potatoes—you can use a vegetable brush to remove the thin skin without damaging the potato. Put the potatoes, whole, in a pot and cover with cold water. Ensure the water level is about an inch above the potatoes. Add a pinch of salt, place the pot over medium-high heat, and bring the water to a boil. Once the water is boiling, reduce the heat to a simmer and cook the potatoes for about 15 to 20 minutes, depending on their size.

Arrange the herring slices in a circle on an oval serving platter, placing two separate bunches of marinated onions in the center, one with red onions, the other with white. Drizzle the herring with sunflower oil, then sprinkle with the spring onions.

Drain the cooked potatoes in a colander. Place them on a deep serving plate, drizzle with 3 tablespoons of sunflower oil, and top with the thin slices of butter so that they melt and coat the potatoes. Chop the dill and sprinkle it over the top. Serve the steaming-hot potatoes and cold Danube herring on their separate serving plates immediately.

Old Odesan Salad with Lightly Salted Mackerel

Nika Lozovska is a globe-trotting young chef—super talented and ambitious—who is among a small number of Ukrainian chefs modernizing the country's cuisine. She has a very popular restaurant in Odesa and, since 2022, has been doing pop-ups across Europe, fundraising for Ukraine. Nika comes from a family of food lovers who have been instrumental in getting her to fall in love with food (see Nika's mum's recipe on page 69). This salad from Nika is a great example of her food philosophy, which she calls "conscious hedonism": enjoying local food to the fullest, ideally in good company and with a glass of Ukrainian wine.

14 oz (400 g) tomatoes

10½ oz (300 g) cucumbers

4 shallots

4 spring onions

A handful of fresh flat-leaf parsley

A handful of fresh dill

10½ oz (300 g) salted mackerel

5¼ oz (150 g) whole olives of choice

5 tablespoons (2½ fl oz/75 ml) sunflower oil

1 tablespoon soy sauce

SERVES 4–6

Cut the tomatoes into wedges. Peel and chop the cucumbers. Thinly slice the shallots. Finely chop the onions, parsley, and dill. Remove the bones and skin from the mackerel, then cut the fillets into bite-size chunks.

In a large serving bowl, combine the tomatoes, cucumbers, shallots, onions, parsley, dill, and mackerel. Gently toss everything together, then add the olives.

In a small bowl, whisk together the sunflower oil and soy sauce until well combined. Drizzle the dressing over the salad, toss lightly, and serve immediately.

Old Odesan Salad with Lightly Salted Mackerel

Pilaf with Mussels

Pilaf with Mussels

To cook mussel pilaf in Odesa, first you need to go to the ferry terminal and buy mussels. They should be large and bluish-black in color and shine like patent-leather shoes. Once you're back home, you need to clean them. Firmly pull the beard from the shells, decisively and without hesitation—even the hungriest cat wouldn't eat that. This is an ideal job for someone in the family who can't hide or pretend to be busy because preparing mussels involves a lot of fuss.

This pilaf recipe comes from Slava, a real Odesan man full of charisma, charm, and generosity. His nickname was Slonik (a little elephant!), maybe because he had such a big heart. Slava built a grill with his own hands in the *dvorik*, or courtyard, of his block of flats. He would fire up this grill even in winter, cooking the most amazing dishes and always inviting lots of friends, family, and even complete strangers. Slava was a proper Odesan host, making everyone feel at home. He played the guitar and had a wicked sense of humor. Slava's *dvorik* with a grill was home to our genuine Odesan spirit. Sadly, Slava passed away in 2022, but his spirit lives on, not the least with this very special recipe.

14 oz (400 g) frozen cooked mussels

18 oz (500 g) fresh mussels

3 onions

4 carrots

3 heads garlic

About ⅔ cup (5 fl oz/150 ml) sunflower oil

Sea salt and freshly ground pepper

2 teaspoons mild chili powder, divided

2 teaspoons ground turmeric

18 oz (500 g) long-grain white rice

About 3 quarts (102 fl oz/3 l) hot water

2 or 3 bay leaves

SERVES 10–12

Thaw the frozen mussels completely for at least 8 hours in the fridge. Before cooking, remove them from the packaging, drain, and set aside.

Put the fresh mussels in a large bowl filled with cold water and scrape off the barnacles with a knife, then remove the beards if needed. Drain.

Heat a large frying pan over high heat. Add the fresh mussels and cook, stirring occasionally, for 3 to 5 minutes, or until the shells have opened. Remove from the heat. Discard any unopened mussels. Do not pour out the juice from the pan; strain it and set aside.

Peel and dice the onions. Peel and cut the carrots into strips. Wash the garlic heads, then carefully cut off the top of the heads so the garlic does not fall apart.

Heat the large casserole over medium heat and pour in the sunflower oil. Add the onions and fry until golden brown. Add the carrots, a pinch of pepper, 1 teaspoon chili powder, and 1 teaspoon turmeric and fry, stirring occasionally, for 10 minutes. Add the thawed mussels and fresh mussels in the shells to the casserole and fry with the onions and carrots, stirring occasionally, for 3 to 4 minutes. Add the rice and garlic and fry, stirring occasionally, for 3 to 4 minutes.

Pour the hot water into the casserole so that it reaches about ½ inch (1.5 cm) above the rice, then pour in the reserved juice from the fresh mussels. Increase the heat to high and bring to a boil. Add salt, pepper, the remaining 1 teaspoon chili powder, the remaining 1 teaspoon turmeric, and bay leaves. Stir the pilaf, reduce the heat to low, cover, and simmer for 25 to 30 minutes, or until the rice is tender. Remove from the heat and let stand in the casserole for another 30 minutes. Stir the pilaf again and remove the bay leaves before serving.

Sandwich with Lightly Salted Black Sea Sprats

Anatoly Modestovich is a legend at Odesa's Privoz Market, where he has been selling fish for some thirty years. Here's his recipe using his beloved sprats. He calls the sandwich "loaders" because sprats are the cheapest of foods, which can so well feed the men working to load and off-load the produce trucks arriving at the market each morning. It's the perfect quick lunch for the workers (and goes especially well with a shot of vodka too). When you buy fresh sprats from one of the stalls, the traders will ask you how salty you want the fish and by the time you get home, voilà, your lunch is ready to eat!

SANDWICHES

9 oz (250 g) fresh sprats or fresh anchovies

Sea salt

½ teaspoon superfine (caster) sugar

1¾ oz (50 g) butter

8 slices rye bread

3 spring onions

SALAD

3 tomatoes

Sea salt

1 red onion

3 tablespoons unrefined sunflower oil

SERVES 4

To prepare the sandwiches, rinse the fish under cold running water and pat dry with paper towels. In a small bowl, mix together 1½ teaspoons salt and the sugar. Sprinkle over the fish and mix well. Cover and refrigerate for 3 to 6 hours.

Using kitchen scissors, cut off the head, then remove the guts from the belly. Open each fish and remove the backbone, then remove the tail. Spread the butter on the bread slices. Place a couple of sprats, skin-side up, on top. Finely chop the spring onions and sprinkle on top of each open sandwich.

To prepare the salad, cut the tomatoes into wedges, place them in a bowl, and season with salt. Cut the red onion into half-rings and layer them on top of the tomatoes. Drizzle with the sunflower oil. Serve the salad alongside the sandwiches.

Sandwich with Lightly Salted Black Sea Sprats

Gefilte Fish

Gefilte Fish

This recipe is particularly special to me, as it comes from my father-in-law, who was quite unwell when we were working on the book but was determined to help preserve the recipe for future generations. His family was Polish Ashkenazi Jewish, and his real name was Eduard Balthasarovich Kalenskyy, which he had to change during Soviet times into a Russified version—Eduart Borisovich—to hide his Polish and Jewish roots. In our family, we have a tradition: Every New Year's Eve, Eduard and his wife, Svetlana, make this gefilte fish for our celebratory table. It's a real treat, as the dish is a labor of love because it takes a good couple of days to prepare. But there would be no festive table for our family without this "golden fish."

7 yellow onions

¾ cup (6.8 fl oz/200 ml) sunflower oil for frying

1 whole carp (about 3 lb 5 oz/1.5 kg)

12 oz pike fillet (350 g)

12 oz zander fillet (350 g)

3½ oz (100 g) white bread roll

5 digestive biscuits

1¼ cups (10 fl oz/300 ml) whole milk

5 eggs

1 tablespoons semolina

Sea salt and freshly ground pepper

Peel the onions, reserving the skins (they will go in the pot when cooking the fish), then dice the onions. Heat the sunflower oil in a large frying pan over medium heat. Add the onions and sauté until deep golden brown. Let cool completely.

Rinse the fish under cold running water. Trim the fins and the tails. Descale each fish and gut it. Remove the gills and eyes. Cut off the head next to the fin area and carefully remove the insides without damaging the gallbladder. Reserve the head.

Gently tap the fish all over with a wooden rolling pin, 8 to 10 times on each side, to loosen the muscles from the skin. Lay the fish, belly-side up, and begin peeling the skin off from the head end, turning it inside out like a stocking. Be careful not to tear the skin. Use scissors to cut the fins from the inside as you go. Near the tail, leave about ¼ inch (5 mm) of meat attached and snap the backbone to remove the skin with the tail intact. Carefully turn the skin inside out and scrape off any remaining meat from the inside with a spoon. Turn the skin back to the right side. Separate all the meat from the bones and reserve the bones (which will go in the pot when cooking the fish). Combine all the meat in a bowl.

CONTINUES ON PAGE 158

FOR THE BED OF VEGETABLES FOR THE FISH

3 beets

3 large carrots

3 yellow onions

4 bay leaves

12 black peppercorns

5 eggs

1 tablespoon semolina

Sea salt and freshly ground black pepper

Boiling water as needed

4 bay leaves

10 black peppercorns

Horseradish sauce

MAKES 1 STUFFED FISH

Meanwhile, in a medium bowl, soak the bread roll and digestive biscuits in the milk.

To prepare the vegetables for the base, peel and slice the beets, carrot, and onions into rounds.

To continue with the fish, pass the fillets and sautéed onions through a meat grinder twice to ensure there are no bone fragments. Place in a large bowl. Remove the soaked roll and biscuits from the milk, reserving the milk. Add the bread and biscuits, eggs, semolina, salt, and pepper to the bowl. Gradually mix together, adding a little of the reserved milk from time to time while stirring constantly to achieve the right consistency. When you reach the consistency of porridge—not so thick that you can't easily stir it—stop adding milk; you may not need all the milk. Beat the stuffing mixture thoroughly by hand. Well-beaten stuffing will turn lighter in color and will easily come off your hands but won't be very thick. Refrigerate the mixture for 30 to 40 minutes.

Meanwhile, wash each fish skin thoroughly. Sew the belly opening closed, leaving one opening unsealed at the head end. Pierce the skin with a needle a few times to allow air to escape during cooking. Carefully fill the fish skin and head with the chilled stuffing, packing it loosely as it will expand as it cooks. Form any leftover stuffing into patties and cook along with the fish.

Remove the rack from a fish-cooking pot. Lay the reserved fish bones and onion skins on the bottom of the pot, then top with the beet, carrot, and onion slices. Replace the rack and place the fish and head on it. Pour boiling water gently into the pot down the sides (not directly on the fish) until it covers the fish completely. Cover the pot with a lid. Bring the water to a boil again over medium-high heat, then add salt, bay leaves, and peppercorns. Reduce the heat to low and simmer the fish for 2 hours.

Carefully remove the fish from the pot, place it on an oval platter, and let cool. When the fish has cooled, carefully remove the string. Chill the fish in the fridge before serving. Assemble the stuffed head back onto the fish for presentation. Cut the fish into slices ½ to ¾ inch (1.5 to 2 cm) thick and serve with horseradish sauce.

NOTE

If you don't have a special pot for stuffed fish (fish poacher), you can use any wide, large pot with a lid. In this case, at first put the fish and its head on the muslin cloth and lay directly on the vegetable base.

Odesan Courtyard Feast

MEATS AND OTHER MAINS

Festive Roast Duck

Festive Roast Duck

When I asked Maria, a founder of Kerkyra Culinary and Wellbeing in Cyprus, what Odesan cuisine meant to her, she simply answered—a celebration! Tables laden with lots of different food, and lots of different people talking, laughing, gossiping, and arguing. Enjoying life! New Year's Eve is the biggest holiday on the calendar in Odesa, when people from all religions, generations, and ethnicities come together and share a feast. Maria tells a story of how she grew up with a tradition of visiting her best friend's family every January 1, where they served this delicate and aromatic duck. New Year's Eve and this duck are the symbols of friendship for Maria. The memory of these festive meals has stayed with her ever since, so she was very happy to re-create this recipe for the book.

1 whole duck,
4½–5½ lb (2–2.5 kg)

3 tablespoons sea salt

3.2 quarts (3 l) boiling water

3 firm apples, such as Granny Smith

GLAZE

Juice of 1 mandarin orange

3 tablespoons cognac

2 tablespoons honey

Sea salt and freshly ground pepper

SERVES 6

Rinse the duck thoroughly and pat dry with paper towels. Trim any excess fat and remove the tail if present. Rub the duck skin generously with the salt and let it stand for 30 minutes. Holding the duck over the sink, carefully pour 6½ cups (1.5 l) of the boiling water evenly over the surface of the duck, making sure not to let any water enter the cavity. The skin will tighten; remove any remaining feathers at this point. Pat dry again with paper towels. Repeat the boiling water rinse and drying process once more. Rub the duck with coarse salt one last time inside and out. Wrap the wings and leg tips in aluminum foil to prevent burning.

Core and cut the apples into large wedges. Fill the duck cavity with the apples, leaving some space to allow air to circulate. Secure the opening with toothpicks or sew it shut with kitchen string.

Preheat the oven to 300°F (150°C).

Position an oven rack in the lower third of the oven, then place the duck, breast-side down, on a foil-lined baking sheet when roasting. Roast for 1½ hours. You will be able to see that the duck has changed color and released a good amount of fat. Increase the oven temperature to 325°F (160°C) and roast for 1 hour more. Increase the oven temperature again to 375°F (190°C). Flip the duck over, breast-side up, and roast for 15 minutes more.

To prepare the glaze, in a small bowl, mix together the mandarin juice, cognac, honey, ½ teaspoon salt, and ½ teaspoon pepper.

Brush the duck with some of the glaze and roast for 5 minutes. Flip the duck over again and brush the other side, then roast for 5 minutes more. Let the duck rest for 10 to 15 minutes before carving. Serve with the roasted apples that were stuffed inside and enjoy the rich, festive flavors of this traditional dish.

NOTE

This dish was always the highlight of our New Year's Day gathering, bringing everyone together around the table. I hope it brings the same warmth and joy to your home!

Sweet and Sour Stew with Prunes

I met Gosha, who shared this recipe, during the days of my cookery school when a good friend of mine dropped by exclaiming, “We’ve got to bring Gosha in! He’ll teach people how to eat well!” And so we did a workshop together, teaching four soups in one go! Gosha comes from an old Jewish family in Odesa and migrated to the United States many years ago. He is not a trained chef but is a great cook and one of those people who “feels food.” He cares a lot about the provenance of ingredients, having made contacts with local farmers and producers in the States, but one thing he still sources only from Odesa is spices. In fact, his friends have devised a method to circumvent the ban of the Ukrainian post on posting unbranded mixes. They attach a made-up brand name and a logo to allow the package for transit! Here’s another example of Odesan creativity and ingenuity. A “slight illegality” as we sometimes call it in Odesa.

3¼ lb (1.5 kg) veal or beef (tenderloin)

3 onions

1 large carrot

10½ oz (300 g) prunes, pitted

About 1 cup (7 fl oz/200 ml) dry red wine

3½ oz (100 g) all-purpose flour

Sea salt and freshly ground pepper

3½ oz (100 g) unsalted butter

5 tablespoons (2½ fl oz/75 ml) sunflower oil, divided

About 1 cup (7 fl oz/200 ml) water, or as needed

About 6 tablespoons (3 fl oz/100 ml) heavy cream

SERVES 6–8

Cut the meat into 2-inch (5-cm) cubes. Peel and finely chop the onions. Peel and coarsely grate the carrot. Rinse the prunes, cut each into 4 pieces, and place in a bowl, then pour in the wine.

Put the flour on a plate. Season the meat with salt and pepper and dredge well in the flour, shaking off the excess. Melt the butter with 2 tablespoons of the sunflower oil in a large frying pan over medium heat. Working in batches as needed, fry the meat in a single layer, taking care not to crowd the pan, until golden brown. Transfer the meat to a large saucepan.

Heat the remaining 3 tablespoons sunflower oil in another large frying pan over low heat. Add the onions and carrot and simmer over low heat until soft. Transfer the vegetables to the saucepan with the meat. Add the 1 cup water (possibly less but not more), cover with a lid, and simmer over low heat, stirring occasionally, for 1 to 3 hours, or until the meat is tender. The cooking time will depend on the quality of the meat.

About 7 minutes before the meat is done, add the prunes and soaking wine to the saucepan. Increase the heat and bring to a boil, then simmer, stirring occasionally.

Finally, pour in the cream, stir, and immediately remove from the heat so the cream does not curdle.

Sweet and Sour Stew with Prunes

Noodly-Stroodly Dumplings with Pork Stew

Noodly-Stroodly Dumplings with Pork Stew

Olga is an artist and rose to prominence through her beautiful drawings of borsch. This recipe for dumplings is one she enjoyed as a little girl whenever she went to stay with her grandmother. There's an ongoing debate, both in their family and in Odesa at large, about the correct name for this dish—some call it strudel, while others call it noodly. But what is clear is that it hails from nineteenth-century Germany, when many Prussians came to settle in Odesa. It's a perfect dish for colder months.

STEW

3¼ lb (1.5 kg) pork neck fillet

3 onions

2 lb (1 kg) potatoes

Sunflower oil for frying

Sea salt and
freshly ground pepper

1 bay leaf

Boiling water as needed

DOUGH

About 1⅓ cups
(11 fl oz/320 ml) kefir

1½ teaspoons sunflower oil

½ teaspoon cider vinegar

1½ teaspoons
superfine (caster) sugar

Sea salt

12 oz (350 g) whole wheat flour,
plus more for dusting

1 teaspoon baking soda

1¾ oz (50 g) butter

Kosher dill pickles

SERVES 10

To prepare the stew, cut the pork into 2-inch (5-cm) pieces. Peel and slice the onions. Peel the potatoes and cut in half if they are large. Leave small potatoes whole.

Heat sunflower oil in a large pot over medium heat. Add the pork pieces and fry until golden brown. Transfer to a plate. Add the onions to the pot and sauté until pale golden brown. Return the meat to the pot and season with salt and pepper. Add the bay leaf and enough boiling water to cover everything. Simmer for about 1 hour, or until the meat is tender, then add the potatoes and cook for 20 minutes.

Meanwhile, prepare the dough: In a large bowl, mix the kefir, sunflower oil, vinegar, sugar, and ½ teaspoon salt. In a medium bowl, stir together the flour and baking soda, then add it to the kefir mixture to form a dough. It should be soft and elastic. Let rest for 20 minutes.

Divide the dough into 2 equal pieces. On a floured surface, roll out each piece 1⁄16 to ⅛ inch (2 to 3 mm) thick. Melt the butter and brush it over the surface of the dough. Roll the buttered dough into a log and cut into 2-inch (5-cm) pieces. Place the dough pieces in a single layer on top of the potatoes, cover tightly with a lid to keep in the steam, and cook over low heat for 20 to 25 minutes. Let the stew and dumplings stand for 15 to 20 minutes before serving. This dish tastes best with pickled or fermented cucumbers.

Chicken Schnitzel "Bitochki"

Odesans are said to be great networkers, in the best definition of this word—we keep connections with our families, friends, colleagues, and neighbors often throughout our lives. These threads continue to weave even when we move thousands of miles away. Lidia, whose recipe this is, left Odesa at the tender age of fifteen, first to New Zealand with her family and later to London to become a top manager in the international bank. But both she and her brother are in close touch with many in their hometown, so much so that even at her brother's wedding in New Zealand, half of the guests had traveled from Pomegranate Street in Odesa! The connections we keep are not just with people; we treasure objects too. So Lidia carries Odesa with her all around the globe, such as an old crystal vase and a lace tablecloth from her family, and an antique ring from her grandmother.

2 boneless, skinless organic chicken breasts, about 14 oz (400 g) total weight

Sea salt and freshly ground pepper

2 tablespoons all-purpose flour

2 eggs

½ cup (4 fl oz/120 ml) sunflower oil

SERVES 4

Cut each chicken breast lengthwise into 2 pieces. Then cut each piece in half to create a total of 8 pieces. Put the chicken pieces on a cutting board, cover with a sheet of parchment paper or plastic wrap, and pound with a rolling pin until they are the same thickness all over. Season with salt and pepper.

Put the flour on a plate and coat each chicken piece on both sides with flour, shaking off any excess. Crack the eggs into a deep plate or shallow bowl, add a pinch of salt, and mix well.

Line a plate with paper towels. Heat the sunflower oil in a large frying pan over medium heat. When the oil is hot, dip each chicken piece into the egg mixture and place it in the pan. Fry the schnitzel for 3 to 4 minutes on each side, or until golden brown. Transfer the schnitzel to the paper towel–lined plate to absorb any excess oil, then serve.

Chicken Schnitzel "Bitochki"

ISOLE

Meat Patties in Batter

Meat Patties in Batter

Lina grew up in a Jewish family of doctors in Odesa and now lives in Berlin. Petite, with an exquisite sense of style and infectious energy, she speaks several languages and travels the world working on all kinds of projects. Lina is nearly eighty and, together with her husband, Fadey, they are my personal example of how to live life to the fullest. This recipe is an ultimate comfort food that comes from the repertoire of dishes that Lina learned to make when she was a young woman. Just after she got married, she began learning how to cook for her husband (a giant man, more than six feet tall!) through her mum's letters, which she has kept to this day. I am so happy that I have Lina and Fadey as my friends, living in the same city (for now at least). This couple is such an inspiration of how to never give up, to continue to learn, to keep moving, to inspire and get inspired. They are a beautiful example of the Odesan wisdom: Don't get fixated on problems, but treat life with humor and kindness.

1 white bread roll (100 g)

About 6 tablespoons (3 fl oz/100 ml) whole milk

2 small onions

12¾ oz (350 g) ground pork

12¾ oz (350 g) ground beef

2 cloves garlic

Sea salt and freshly ground pepper

2 eggs

3 tablespoons all-purpose flour

Sunflower oil for frying

SERVES 4–6

Put the bread roll in a small bowl, pour in the milk, and let soak. Peel and finely chop the onions. In a large bowl, mix together the ground pork and beef, then grate in the garlic. Thoroughly mash the bread roll with a fork and add it to the meat mixture. Then add the onions, season with salt and pepper, and mix the meat thoroughly with a fork until it becomes easy to shape into balls.

In a bowl, lightly beat the eggs with a fork, add the flour and 1 teaspoon salt, and mix until a smooth batter forms.

Heat sunflower oil in a large frying pan over medium heat. Reduce the heat to low. Using a tablespoon, scoop out the meat mixture and shape with your hands into a round, flat patty. Using a fork, dip each patty into the batter, coating both sides, then place in the frying pan. You will have about 20 patties total. Working in batches as needed, fry the patties for 4 minutes on each side. Transfer the patties to a deep bowl and cover to keep warm, then let them rest for 5 minutes before serving.

Toasted Porridge à la Odesan Beach

Most of us from the former Soviet Union grew up with semolina porridge. It's a dish of simple beauty—very smooth, no lumps, please. Katerina and her family have German roots. Historically many Germans in Odesa were engineers, like Katerina's great-grandfather, who was a famous engineer. Katerina has become one of the best-known and talented tour guides in Odesa. She shows people many hidden corners of the city, including *dvoriks*, or courtyards. Her dad, who was born in a house with just such a *dvorik*, gave us this lovely recipe, which he inherited through the German line of his family. He dry-fries the grains first, creating a caramelized, toffee-like flavor. I love how the semolina ends up looking like the sand on Odesan beaches.

1½ cups (12 fl oz/350 ml) water
3½ oz (100 g) semolina
1¾ oz (50 g) butter, divided
Sea salt

SERVES 2

Pour the water into a saucepan and bring to a boil over high heat.

Meanwhile, heat a dry deep frying pan over medium heat. Add the semolina and toast, stirring constantly to prevent burning, until it turns a light golden color.

Once the semolina reaches the right shade, carefully pour in half of the boiling water and immediately cover the pan with a lid for a few seconds. Be careful, as the hot grains will sputter and may jump out of the pan. A deeper frying pan is preferable to keep the stovetop clean. Reduce the heat to low, add half of the butter, and season with salt. Pour in the remaining boiling water and simmer, stirring vigorously to prevent lumps, for 3 to 5 minutes, or until the porridge begins to "puff." Add the remaining butter and serve immediately.

NOTE

The longer you fry the semolina, the darker its color will be and the richer the flavor will become. Fried semolina porridge can be served as a separate dish or as a side dish to a stew.

Toasted Porridge à la Odesan Beach

ДУХИ
Англiйскiе и французскiе
О-Де-Колонъ
ПОМАДА, ПУДРА
ЛУЧШИХЪ ФАБРИКЪ
КРАСКА ВОЛОСЪ
СРЕДСТВА
КО

Tiered Liver Cake with Caramelized Onions

Tiered Liver Cake with Caramelized Onions

Zhenya grew up in a quintessential Odesan communal flat; his own family and most neighbors were Jewish. This recipe belongs to Zhenya's mum Natalya Shaevna. She would make this savory cake for all special occasions, and it was his favorite. Natalya was one of those super women, managing a successful career, raising two sons, and making fresh meals every day, catering for dietary requirements of each family member! She would often get up at 5 a.m. to go to the Privoz Market before work to buy all the ingredients and then cook when she was back home in the evening. Sometimes she would take little Zhenya with her to the market, teaching him how to buy ingredients well and how to sample food. To this day he never buys at a market without tasting first.

Natalya was a collector of cookbooks, but her own book of recipes has unfortunately been lost, so I have helped Zhenya and her restore this recipe using the knowledge of the older generation of women in Odesa.

5 onions

Sunflower oil for frying

About 2 tablespoons butter

Sea salt and
freshly ground pepper

24½ oz (700 g) chicken livers

2 eggs

About 1 cup (7 fl oz/200 ml)
whole milk

5¼ oz (150 g) all-purpose flour

⅓ bunch fresh dill

9 oz (250 g) mayonnaise

SERVES 8

Peel and slice the onions into half-rings. Heat sunflower oil in a large frying pan over medium heat. Add the onions and fry until golden brown, adding the butter and a pinch of salt halfway through. Let the onions cool.

Meanwhile, blend the chicken livers in a food processor or pass them through a meat grinder. In a large bowl, whisk together the eggs, milk, 1 teaspoon salt, and ½ teaspoon pepper. Gradually add the flour while stirring to prevent any lumps. Add the chicken livers and mix well.

Heat a 9½-inch (24-cm) frying pan over medium heat and grease it lightly with sunflower oil. Pour in a thin layer of batter and cook for 2 to 3 minutes on each side. Repeat to cook a total of 9 pancakes. Let them cool.

Finely chop the dill. Place a pancake on a serving plate, spread some mayonnaise on it, and sprinkle with some of the fried onions. Repeat the layering with the remaining pancakes, mayonnaise, and fried onions. Garnish with the dill and refrigerate for at least 2 hours before serving.

Aunty Beba's Stuffed Zucchini

"I was the first one to say I was Jewish out loud," Inna Emilievna Rikun-Stein told us as she recalled her career as a librarian. Inna is a fount of knowledge when it comes to Odesa's history. She explained how during Soviet times, many people were forced to change their names, hide their ethnicity, and avoid using their language. But the food that people cooked at home revealed who they truly were. This recipe is the epitome of late summer in Odesa and belongs to Inna's mother, who was famous for both her food and her generosity.

3½ oz (100 g) short-grain white rice

Boiling water as needed

18 oz (500 g) boneless, skinless organic chicken breasts

2 onions

2 large carrots

½ bunch fresh flat-leaf parsley, divided

½ bunch fresh dill, divided

6 zucchini

6 tomatoes

Sunflower oil for frying

1¾ tablespoons butter

Sea salt and freshly ground pepper

1 teaspoon superfine (caster) sugar

5¼ oz (150 g) sour cream

SERVES 6

In a bowl, soak the rice in boiling water for 30 minutes and then drain. Cut the chicken into very small cubes. Peel and finely chop the onions. Peel and coarsely grate the carrots. Finely chop the parsley and dill. Cut each zucchini in half lengthwise and hollow out each half with a tablespoon to make 2 "cups." You will have a total of 12. Reserve the scraped-out zucchini flesh. Grate the tomatoes into a deep bowl, discarding the skins.

Heat sunflower oil in a large frying pan over medium heat. Add the onions and sauté until translucent. Add the carrots and butter, reduce the heat to low, and cook for 10 minutes. Heat sunflower oil in another large frying pan over medium heat. Add the chicken and lightly fry until golden.

In a large bowl, mix together the chicken, rice, sautéed onions and carrots, and half each of the parsley and dill. Season with salt and pepper. Stuff the zucchini "cups" with the filling. In a medium bowl, mix together the tomatoes and sugar, and season with salt and pepper.

Spread the reserved zucchini flesh evenly on the bottom of a wide, deep frying pan. Arrange the stuffed zucchini tightly in the pan and pour over the tomato sauce. Cover with a lid and cook over low heat for 30 to 40 minutes, or until the zucchini are tender. Serve with sour cream and sprinkle with the remaining dill and parsley.

NOTE

You can make a vegetarian version by omitting the meat and increasing the amount of rice, onions, and carrots. For this amount of zucchini, use 7 oz (200 g) rice, 4 onions, and 4 carrots. Inna, who's from a Jewish family, prepares these stuffed zucchini with chicken, while I prefer them with a 50-50 mix of ground pork and beef—this makes them even juicier!

Aunty Beba's Stuffed Zucchini

ФРЭШ
PRODUCT OF ECUADOR

"Bulgarian" Stuffed Peppers

"Bulgarian" Stuffed Peppers

Bessarabia is part of the Odesan region. This ancient region of vineyards, fertile land, and lots of sunshine has changed its shape and many hands over the centuries, currently with two-thirds being in Moldova and the rest in southwestern Ukraine. This recipe comes from Dima Sikorskij, a restaurateur with Polish roots, an interior designer, and a food anthropologist of sorts who has spearheaded the interest and research into Bessarabian and Odesan food and wine culture in Ukraine.

One of Dima's best-known restaurants was a bodega called Two Karls, located in one of the oldest houses in the city that has always been home to an eating establishment of some kind. "Let's meet at the corner of two Karls" was a popular phrase, as the house was on the corner of two streets: one named after Karl Marx and the other after Karl Liebknecht, both revolutionists. This recipe from Dima is a great example of a Bessarabian dish that highlights the multinational mix of the area: sweet or bell peppers are called "Bulgarian" in this part of Ukraine to reference the Bulgarian traders who would often sell peppers at Odesan markets, and stuffing vegetables is such a Greek tradition.

8 large red or yellow bell peppers

STUFFING

7 oz (200 g) long-grain white rice

Boiling water as needed

2 large onions

1 large carrot

⅓ cup (2¾ fl oz/80 ml) sunflower oil

19½ oz (550 g) ground pork

Sea salt and freshly ground pepper

TOMATO SAUCE

2 large onions

1 large carrot

5 tomatoes

About 3½ tablespoons sunflower oil

3 bay leaves

1 teaspoon peppercorns

Sea salt

5¼ oz (150 g) sour cream

SERVES 6–8

Cut the tops off the bell peppers and carefully remove the seeds. Set the peppers and the cutoff tops aside.

To make the stuffing, put the rice in a bowl and pour in boiling water to cover the rice completely. Let stand for 10 minutes, then drain. Peel and finely dice the onions. Peel and coarsely grate the carrot. Heat the sunflower oil in a large frying pan over medium heat. Add the onions and fry until transparent. Add the carrot and fry for 10 minutes. In a large bowl, combine rice, ground pork, onions, and carrot. Season with salt and pepper and mix.

To make the tomato sauce, peel and finely dice the onions. Peel and coarsely grate the carrot. Finely dice the tomatoes. Heat the sunflower oil in a large frying pan over medium heat. Add the onions and fry until transparent. Add the carrot and fry for 5 minutes. Add the tomatoes and sauté for 5 minutes. Remove from the heat.

Fill each bell pepper with the stuffing and cover with the cutoff top. Stand the stuffed peppers in a pot just large enough to hold them in a single layer without crowding. Carefully pour in the sauce and then pour in enough water to cover the peppers almost completely. Add the bay leaves and peppercorns and season with salt.

Set the pot over medium heat, cover with a lid, and bring to a boil. Reduce the heat to medium-low and simmer for 35 to 40 minutes, or until the peppers are soft and the stuffing is no longer pink in the center. Serve the peppers immediately with the tomato sauce over the top and with sour cream.

Armenian Lamb Stew Khashlama

Bella, who comes from an Armenian family, shared her favorite recipe, which was passed on to her by her father, Arthur. He always used the same knife for this dish, and Bella continues to make it using that same knife. The dish relies on very good ingredients, as there's no room to hide. When we prepared it together, we headed out to the Privoz Market to buy the best lamb and vegetables. You need a fattier cut of meat so that the flavor gradually gets released into the stew while it cooks for several hours. It's a generous, heartwarming dish, just like Bella herself.

2 lb (1 kg) young lamb (mix of shoulder and leg steak)

4 large onions

4 tomatoes

5 large potatoes

1 red bell pepper

1 chile pepper

½ bunch fresh cilantro

Sea salt

Crusty bread

SERVES 4–6

Cut the lamb into 2½-inch (6-cm) pieces. Peel the onions and slice them into rings. Cut the tomatoes into slices ⅜ inch (1 cm) thick. Peel the potatoes and cut them into wedges. Remove the seeds from the bell pepper and slice it into strips. Roughly chop the chile pepper and cilantro.

In a large saucepan, layer the ingredients in the following order: onions, lamb, salt, tomatoes, potatoes, salt, chile pepper, a few strips of bell pepper, and some of the cilantro. Repeat the layers in the same order, generously salting each meat and potato layer.

Add a little water to the pan so it is about one-third full, cover with the lid, and bring to a boil. Reduce the heat to low and simmer gently without stirring for about 2 hours, or until the meat is tender. Serve with crusty bread to mop up the delicious juices.

Armenian Lamb Stew Khashlama

Dacha Chicken Pilaf

Dacha Chicken Pilaf

This is a story of how you can take the girl out of Odesa, but you can't take Odesa out of the girl. When Anna was 2, her whole family moved to Germany, including her grandparents and great-grandfather. The family's roots were Jewish, and Germany was welcoming members of the Jewish diaspora from around the world. Despite the big move, Anna's grandparents remained very active participants of Ukrainian and Odesan émigré life in Berlin. Anna's Grandpa Valik was the head of the Club of the Odesans for many years, giving lectures on the history and art of his hometown.

At home, her Grandma Galina cooked a variety of *dacha* dishes, including this wonderful pilaf. There is a whole collection of special dishes in Ukraine that people cook during the warmer months, when they move from their homes in the city to their *dacha*, or summer cottage. This is a lot less luxurious than it might seem (see my notes on the *dacha* phenomenon), especially since *dacha*s were often very basic dwellings. Sometimes they didn't even have running water or electricity, but they always had nature all around. Now that Anna has her own young daughter, she feeds her this delicious pilaf, passing on the memories of her Odesan life.

2 lb (1 kg) onions

21 oz (600 g) carrots

3¼ lb (1.5 kg) boneless, skinless organic chicken breasts or thighs

2 lb (1 kg) long-grain white rice

1 head garlic

Sunflower oil for frying

1 teaspoon ground cumin

Sea salt and freshly ground pepper

SERVES 10

Peel and chop the onions. Peel and cut the carrots into thick strips. Cut the chicken into medium-size pieces. Rinse the rice thoroughly under running cold water until the water runs clear. Wash the garlic head, then remove the outer layer of skin but don't peel the cloves.

Heat sunflower oil in a deep pot over medium heat. Add the onions and fry until golden, then add the chicken and continue frying until the chicken starts to brown, about 5 minutes. Add the carrots and cook for 4 to 5 minutes, stirring constantly so they don't stick to the pan. Pour in enough water to cover the ingredients. Reduce the heat, add the cumin, and season with salt and pepper. Simmer for 40 to 50 minutes.

Layer the rice on top and pour in more water so it covers the rice by about ¾ inch (2 cm). Gently press the garlic head into the center of the rice. Bring to a rapid boil and boil until the water evaporates, then cover with a lid, reduce the heat to low, and cook for 25 to 30 minutes. Don't stir during this time. Remove from the heat and let the pilaf rest, covered, for 10 minutes. Mix everything thoroughly together and serve hot, garnished with the softened garlic cloves if desired.

Ukrainian Dumplings Varenyky

Nadya Kulakovska and the other women regularly cook together in the old Odesan yard in Moldavanka. They pass on the traditions to their children and the friends of their children from the whole area. The *varenyky* are considered by many to be a national dish: pliable dough rolled by hand, cut into circles, and stuffed with all manner of delicious things, then briefly boiled and eaten with big helpings of sour cream and fried onions.

POTATO FILLING

21 oz (600 g) potatoes

Sea salt

2 onions

¼ cup (2 fl oz/60 ml) plus 3 tablespoons sunflower oil, divided

Freshly ground pepper

CABBAGE FILLING

¼ to ⅓ (400 g) medium white cabbage

5 tablespoons sunflower oil, divided

1 carrot

2 onions

Sea salt and freshly ground pepper

DOUGH

1 egg

2 tablespoons sunflower oil

½ teaspoon sea salt

12¾ oz (360 g) all-purpose flour

About 1 cup (7 fl oz/200 ml) boiling water

FOR SERVING

1¾ oz (50 g) butter

7 oz (200 g) sour cream

MAKES 40–50

To prepare the potato filling, peel the potatoes and cut them into halves or quarters, depending on their size. Put them in a large saucepan, cover with water, and add salt. Bring to a boil over high heat, then reduce the heat to low and simmer for 20 to 25 minutes, or until tender. Drain the potatoes and mash until smooth.

Peel and dice the onions. Heat the sunflower oil in a large frying pan over low heat. Add the onions and fry for 5 to 7 minutes, or until golden brown. Set aside half of the fried onions for garnish. Add the remaining fried onions and their frying oil to the bowl with the mashed potatoes and stir. Season with salt and pepper.

To prepare the cabbage filling, shred the cabbage into a large bowl and toss it gently with your hands. Heat 3 tablespoons of the sunflower oil in a large, deep frying pan over low heat. Add the cabbage, stirring so it is evenly covered with the oil. Cover with a lid and simmer for 7 to 10 minutes, or until soft.

Peel and coarsely grate the carrot. Add to the pan with the cabbage, then cover and simmer for 10 minutes. Peel and dice the onions. Set aside half of the onions. Add the remaining onions to the vegetables in the pan and mix. Cover and simmer for 10 minutes. Season with salt and pepper to taste. Transfer the cabbage filling to a large plate to cool. Heat the frying pan over low heat, add the remaining 2 tablespoons sunflower oil, and when it's hot, fry the reserved onions for 5 to 7 minutes, or until golden brown. Set aside for garnish.

To make the dough, combine the egg, sunflower oil, and salt in a bowl and beat a little with a whisk. Add the flour and stir. While stirring, gradually pour in the boiling water. Knead the dough until it becomes soft and does not stick to your hands. Form it into a ball, cover with a kitchen towel, and let stand for 10 minutes. Roll out the dough to a thickness of 1⁄16 inch (2 mm). Using a glass, cut the dough into circles.

Place a full teaspoon of the filling of choice in the center of each dough circle, fold into a half-moon shape, and crimp or pleat the edges.

Bring a large saucepan of water to a boil over high heat and add salt. Once it comes to a rolling boil, throw in the dumplings and immediately stir so they don't stick to the bottom. Melt the butter and pour into a large serving bowl. Cook the dumplings for 3 to 4 minutes, then drain well. Transfer the dumplings to the bowl with the butter and swirl them around. Serve with sour cream and the reserved fried onions.

Ukrainian Dumplings Varenyky

Moldavian Polenta Mamalyga

Moldavian Polenta Mamalyga

Misha, a well-known musician, and his mother, Nina, are descended from the aristocratic Greek family of Ksida from the island of Chios. Fearing the threat of the Ottoman Empire, their ancestors left the island and came to Odesa, where they built a successful grain-trading business. But after the 1917 revolution, the business and all the family's wealth were lost. Most of the family emigrated to escape the Bolshevik regime, but a few stayed in Ukraine and moved to a predominantly Moldovan village near Odesa. During Soviet times the family had to hide their Greek origins, and so Moldovan dishes became the household staples. Mamalyga is an iconic Moldovan dish, normally eaten hot, but Misha suggests slicing up the cooled corn polenta, then serving it with chopped-up vegetables and cheese. Delicious.

7 oz (200 g) smoked bacon lardons

3½ oz (100 g) salty sheep's milk cheese or Ukrainian brynza

1 head garlic

About 6 tablespoons (3 fl oz/100 ml) sunflower oil

2¾ cups (22 fl oz/650 ml) water, divided

Sea salt

10½ oz (300 g) coarse polenta

1¾ oz (50 g) butter

SERVES 4

Fry the bacon lardons in a dry frying pan over low heat for 15 minutes, or until crispy. Transfer to a bowl.

Grate the cheese into another bowl. Separate the garlic cloves, then crush them into a third bowl. Pour in the sunflower oil and ¼ cup (2 fl oz/50 ml) of the water. Season with salt and mix well.

Fill a large saucepan with the remaining 2½ cups (20 fl oz/600 ml) water, season with salt, and bring to a boil over high heat. Reduce the heat to low and add the polenta in a slow, continuous stream, stirring constantly with a wooden spoon. Simmer, stirring constantly, for about 10 minutes, then reduce the heat as low as possible. Add the butter and simmer, stirring occasionally so the polenta doesn't stick to the pan, for about 20 minutes, or until the polenta is creamy and the grains are tender.

Remove from the heat. Turn the polenta (mamalyga) out onto a plate and cut it. Then pinch a little bit with your fingers and dip it into the lardons, cheese, or garlic oil.

NOTE

Brynza is our most popular and best-loved type of cheese. It can be made from cow's or sheep's milk or a mix of the two. In Bessarabia people prefer the saltier and more intense sheep milk's version, but in Odesa, we hanker after what we call "sweet brynza"—a delicate, creamy version made with cow's milk. Crusty bread with a thick layer of freshly churned butter and a slice of brynza, alongside a cup of sweet black tea, is the best breakfast you can imagine.

A few years ago, I organized a panel discussion in Odesa about our local ingredients including, of course, brynza cheese. Among the panelists were two foreign chefs, one from Italy and another from France. I asked them why they chose to live and work in Odesa. After all, they came from countries famed for the quality of their fresh produce, cheese, and other foods. "Tomatoes and brynza," they replied in unison.

Finger-Size Stuffed Cabbage Leaf Rolls

These cabbage rolls can be found all over Ukraine, but in Odesa they are often made more dainty, or "one-biters," as we like to say. I was taught this recipe by Elena Radchenko, who had learned it from her grandma. Elena moves very quickly when she is cooking—it really is a wonder to watch. She manages to combine looking after a big family and running a successful business.

The classic version of cabbage leaf rolls uses pork instead of turkey and short-grain rice instead of bulgur. For extra richness, you can layer the stuffed cabbage rolls with pieces of butter. On special occasions, the bottom of the saucepan (*kazan*) is lined with cabbage leaves, followed by layers of fried bone-in meat with golden brown onions or smoked ribs, then the cabbage rolls. During cooking, the cabbage absorbs the meat's aroma. When serving, the saucepan can be turned over onto a deep serving dish, then the meat is resting beautifully on top of the cabbage rolls.

CABBAGE ROLLS

1 cabbage, 2–2¾ lb (1–1.5 kg)

Sea salt and freshly ground pepper

Juice of ½ lemon

3½ oz (100 g) bulgur

Boiling water as needed

2 carrots

1 onion

1 zucchini

10½ oz (300 g) ground turkey

10½ oz (300 g) ground beef

4 cloves garlic

5¼ oz (150 g) cherry tomatoes

To prepare the cabbage rolls, remove the cabbage leaves, wash them, and cut out the core and any tough parts. Fill a large saucepan with water and add a pinch of salt and the lemon juice; this helps the leaves stay elastic. Bring the water to a boil over high heat, add the cabbage leaves, and blanch for 5 to 10 minutes, depending on the variety. The leaves should become soft and slightly translucent. As they start to separate, transfer them one by one to a bowl and let cool. Smooth leaves are needed for stuffed cabbage rolls. The central part of the cabbage is not suitable for stuffing; save it to use later (see Note).

Soak the bulgur in boiling water for 5 minutes, then drain. Peel the carrots and onion and grate them with a medium grater. Grate the zucchini, then mix it with the carrots and onion in a medium bowl. In a large bowl, combine the ground meats, the vegetable mixture, bulgur, 1 teaspoon salt, and ½ teaspoon pepper and mix well.

Preheat the oven to 350°F (180°C).

Cut each cabbage leaf in half, removing the thick central rib. Then cut each large half into 2 smaller triangle-shaped pieces. Gently pound any thick parts of the leaves to make them more flexible. Place 1 teaspoon of the meat filling along one edge of the cabbage leaf and carefully roll it around the filling, turning it once as you roll, so it forms a cone shape. There will be a wider opening at the top; tuck in the edges like an envelope so the filling is neatly sealed inside. Repeat with the remaining cabbage leaves and filling.

CONTINUES ON PAGE 200

SAUCE

About 2¼ cups (17 fl oz/500 ml) water

¼ cup (2 oz/60 g) tomato paste

About ¾ cup (7 fl oz/200 ml) cream

2 teaspoons sweet paprika

Sea salt

5¼ oz (150 g) sour cream

A handful of fresh flat-leaf parsley, roughly chopped

SERVES 6–8 (MAKES 40–50 ROLLS)

Peel and slice the garlic and halve the tomatoes. Arrange the stuffed cabbage rolls tightly in a wide, shallow, oven-safe saucepan, layering them with the garlic and tomatoes.

To prepare the sauce, in a bowl, mix together the water, tomato paste, and cream. Add the sweet paprika, season with salt, and stir well. Pour the sauce over the cabbage rolls.

Place the uncovered saucepan in the oven for 10 minutes, allowing the sauce to come to a boil. Then cover the pan with a lid and continue cooking in the oven for 1½ hours, or until the cabbage is soft, uncovering the pan during the last 10 minutes of cooking.

Serve the stuffed cabbage rolls hot with the sour cream and sprinkled with the parsley.

NOTE

In Odesa, a good cook makes sure nothing goes to waste. After blanching and trimming the cabbage leaves, you will have leftover scraps and extra leaves. Some can be placed on the bottom of the saucepan before adding the cabbage rolls, while others can be used to cover the rolls on top—why throw them away?

In winter, we often make stuffed cabbage rolls using fermented (sour) cabbage. Before cooking, soak the whole head of cabbage overnight in water with 1½ teaspoons baking soda, which will make the cabbage softer and less salty and sour. Rinse the cabbage, separate the leaves, and trim the thick parts. Reduce the salt in the recipe by one-third. Fermented cabbage will also cook faster.

Finger-Size Stuffed Cabbage Leaf Rolls

Stuffed Chicken Neck

Stuffed Chicken Neck

This is a dish that, undeniably, requires a lot of patience, but the result is spectacular, with a delicious mousse-like filling made from delicate chicken livers and other parts, plus sweet onions and eggs. The recipe comes from my mother-in-law, Natalia, whose ancestors were Greek from the island of Santorini.

Natalia recalls that, when she was growing up, one chicken could be turned into at least five dishes, feeding a family for at least two days! The breast was made into little patties, while the offal with a bit of meat, flour, and chicken fat became the filling for the neck. The thighs were stuffed with whatever was at hand and pan-fried. The skin was chopped up and fried, a bit like bacon—called *schkvarki.* Then the bones, any leftover meat scraps, and the chicken feet and combs were used to prepare the most amazing broth. It's real, no-waste cooking, Odesa style.

1 whole chicken, 4½–5½ lb (2–2.5 kg)

2 lb (1 kg) onions

About 6 tablespoons (3 fl oz/100 ml) sunflower oil

10½ oz (300 g) chicken hearts

10½ oz (300 g) chicken stomachs

10½ oz (300 g) chicken livers

8 eggs

7–9 oz (200–250 g) semolina (see Note)

Sea salt and freshly ground pepper

2 bay leaves

SERVES 4–6

Wash the chicken thoroughly. Cut off the lower portion of the legs. Carefully separate the skin from the meat using your hands. Remove the legs one at a time through the large opening, reaching toward the wings. Put the leg meat aside to use later for another dish. Trim the inside of the chicken, ensuring it is clean. Continue peeling the skin from the wings. Once the chicken is fully cleaned, sew up all the holes, leaving only one opening at one leg, which will be used for filling with the stuffing. Reserve the chicken skin.

Peel the onions, reserving the skins, then dice the onions. Heat the sunflower oil in a large frying pan over medium heat. Add the onions and fry until golden brown.

Meanwhile, bring a large saucepan of water to a boil over high heat. Add the chicken hearts and stomachs and boil, then transfer to a cutting board and cut into small cubes. Dice the raw chicken livers and breast.

In a large bowl, combine the fried onions, chicken hearts, stomachs, livers, and breast, the eggs, and semolina, adding enough semolina to create a pourable mixture. Season the stuffing mixture with salt and pepper.

CONTINUES ON PAGE 204

Bring a pot of salted water to a boil over high heat. Meanwhile, lay a piece of muslin on a cutting board and place the reserved chicken skin on top. Using a funnel, fill the chicken with the stuffing mixture through the leg opening. While stuffing the chicken, try to expel as much air as possible. Do not fill it too tightly, as the stuffing will expand when the chicken is boiled and this may rip the skin. Once filled, sew up the leg opening to secure the stuffing inside. Pierce the chicken in several places with a needle to release any remaining air. Loosely tie the muslin with the skin crosswise around the chicken.

Place the muslin-wrapped chicken into the pot of boiling water and add the bay leaves along with the reserved onion skins, which will give the chicken a beautiful color. Cook for 1½ hours, then carefully turn the chicken over and cook for another 1½ hours.

Remove the chicken from the pot and place on a plate. Carefully untie the muslin and turn the chicken onto another dish to preserve its shape and appearance. Refrigerate until chilled, then remove the strings and serve.

NOTE

The quantity of semolina depends on the size of the chicken and the volume and fluidity of your mixture. It's important to keep the mixture pourable, as you will use a funnel to fill the chicken.

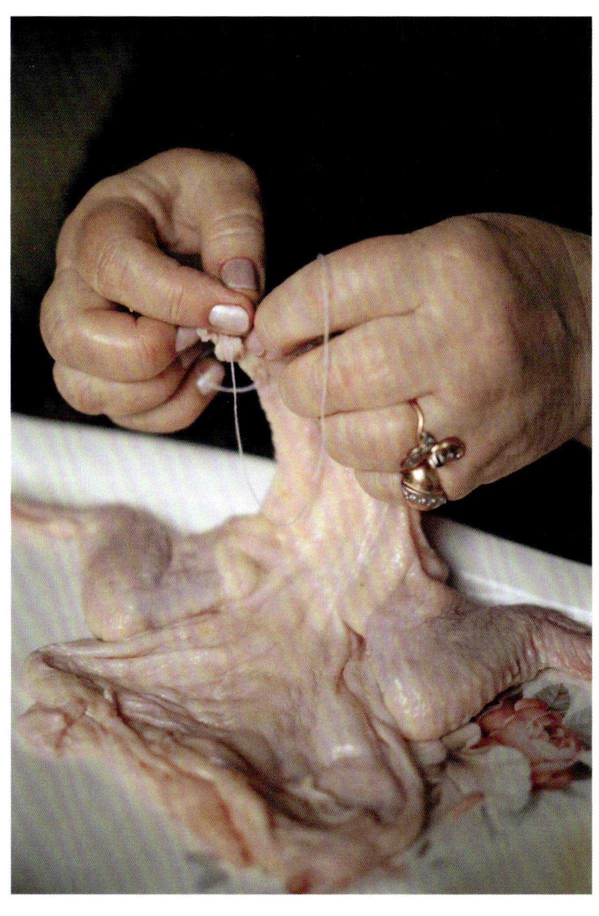

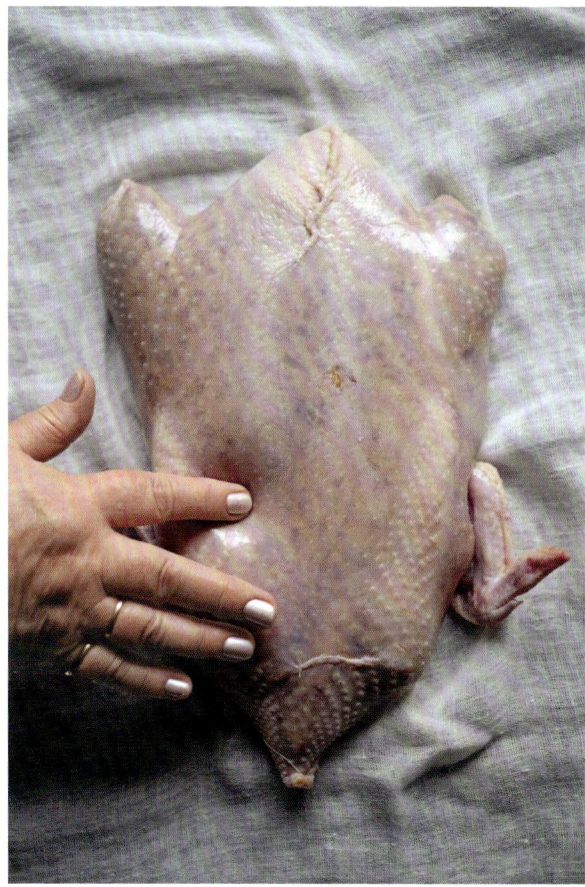

BANANAS

From the Garden

FERMENTING, PICKLING, AND PRESERVING

Pickled Watermelon

Pickled Watermelon

Sabina is a popular Odesan family photographer. She loves people, which is why they always appear so beautifully in her pictures. Sabina's mother, who is a manager at Odesa's central train station, is famous for her fermented watermelons. When the season starts, even if she's incredibly busy, she takes time off to ferment them. These watermelons are always an important feature at family gatherings. Paradoxically, the first time Sabina sampled her mum's watermelons was when she made them for this book—until then, other people always managed to eat them before she could get her hands on any!

4½ lb (2 kg) watermelon
1 rib celery with leaves
2 cloves garlic
¼ red chile, sliced
5 peppercorns
2 bay leaves
Boiling water as needed
2 tablespoons sugar
Sea salt
3 tablespoons cider vinegar

MAKES ONE 3-QUART (102-FL OZ/3-L) JAR

Cut the watermelon into slices ¾ inch (2 cm) thick, leaving the rind on. Cut each slice into triangular wedges. Put the celery, garlic, chile, peppercorns, and bay leaves into a sterilized 3-quart (102-fl oz/3-l) jar with a lid (see page 241). Put all the watermelon pieces into the jar and pour in boiling water to cover the watermelon. Cover with the lid and let stand for 10 minutes.

Drain the water from the jar into a saucepan, then bring it to a boil over high heat and pour over the watermelon again. Cover with the lid and let stand for another 10 minutes. Drain the water into the saucepan again and bring to a boil. Meanwhile, add the sugar, 1 tablespoon salt, and the vinegar to the jar, then pour in the boiling water for the third time. Close the lid tightly and turn the jar upside down. Cover the jar with a blanket and let stand at room temperature for 2 days. Then transfer the jar to the fridge. The pickled watermelon will be ready in 1 month.

Angela's Famous Tomatoes with Garlic and Herbs

Angela has always been a great cook, but she never thought of having a career in food. Instead, she had run a successful fashion business in Ukraine for years. One day, she was on the beach (a lot happens on the beach in Odesa—we spend almost half a year there!), where she met Inga, another passionate home cook. Their conversation about recipes, ingredients, and markets led them to opening the first chain of delis in the city that served authentic Odesan cuisine. Mama Choli quickly became a hit, celebrating the real, home-cooked food of Odesa.

1 large head garlic

1 bunch fresh dill

1 bunch fresh flat-leaf parsley

1 bunch fresh basil

4½ lb (2 kg) tomatoes

About 1 quart (34 fl oz/1 l) water

About 6 tablespoons (3 fl oz/100 ml) cider vinegar

2½ oz (75 g) sugar

Sea salt

1½ oz (40 g) mixed peppercorns

2 small chiles

SERVES 4–6

Peel and finely chop the garlic. Roughly chop the dill, parsley, and basil. Peel the tomatoes, which is easily done by cutting a small cross at the base of each one, then plunging them into boiling water for about 20 seconds. When cool enough to handle, peel the tomatoes.

In a large saucepan, bring the water to a boil over high heat. Add the vinegar, sugar, 2 tablespoons salt, and peppercorns, then remove the marinade from the heat.

In a large bowl or wide jar, start with a layer of herbs and all the garlic, then the tomatoes. Pile the remaining herbs and the chiles on top. Pour over the hot marinade. Cover and let stand at room temperature for 24 hours, then place in the fridge. The tomatoes will keep in the fridge for up to 1 month.

Angela's Famous Tomatoes with Garlic and Herbs

5 6 7
8 9 10

Red Tomato Juice

Red Tomato Juice

I think tomato juice is a lot more popular in Ukraine and Eastern Europe than in the UK or America (and not as part of a cocktail!). Children often drink it alongside a meal. In Natalia's family this thick, sweet-and-sour juice is one of their favorite drinks. She grows a certain variety of tomatoes at her little summer cottage specifically for making the juice. Every August and September she harvests tomatoes when they're very ripe and bottles many liters of juice. Her daughter, who now lives in Vienna and has traveled the world as a travel blogger, loves the stuff and always takes a few bottles back home whenever she visits.

11 lb (5 kg) plum tomatoes
Sugar (see Note)
Sea salt (see Note)

MAKES FIVE 3-CUP (24-FL OZ/700-ML) BOTTLES

Cut each tomato into quarters. Using a cold-press juicer, squeeze the juice from the tomatoes and pour into a large saucepan.

Place the saucepan over medium heat and bring the tomato juice to a boil. Reduce the heat and simmer for 20 minutes, making sure any foam has subsided. Add sugar and salt to taste and stir.

Remove the pan from the heat. While the juice is still hot, pour it into five 3-cup (24–fl oz/700-ml) sterilized bottles (see page 241) and turn the screw caps on tightly to seal. Place the bottles horizontally on a towel so they don't slide around and let cool. Store the juice in the fridge for up to 3 months.

NOTE

You can use any quantity of tomatoes for this recipe. An average of 3 to 3¼ lb (1.35 to 1.5 kg) of tomatoes are needed to make about 1 quart (34 fl oz/1 l) of juice. The most delicious juice is made from ripe seasonal tomatoes. The amount of salt and sugar added to the juice depends on the type of tomato and its natural sweetness and saltiness. For flavor, you can also add allspice to the juice before cooking; use 3 to 4 teaspoons per 11 lb (5 kg) of tomatoes.

Lightly Salted Fermented Cucumbers

As a lecturer at Odesa National Technological University and a restaurant consultant, Katerina gave many Odesan chefs a head start. She chose these lightly salted cucumbers to include in this book, as they reminded her of the carefree days she spent in a summerhouse by the sea. Rodnichok, the name of the cucumber variety, means the ones close to your heart, homeland, or family. You can find these petite, aromatic cucumbers in almost every Odesan kitchen at the height of the season. They are incredibly tasty eaten alongside crispy fried potatoes and eggs for breakfast. Or snacking on them as you might enjoy popcorn, which I did as a little girl while wandering through Odesa's markets. The brine can be refrigerated and reused several times by adding a little more salt. Look for small, prickly cucumbers in Eastern European shops in the UK and abroad. If they aren't available, use regular cucumbers (but only if you really have to!).

2 lb (1 kg) small cucumbers, such as Rodnichok

Fine sea salt

1½ tablespoons honey

About 1 quart (34 fl oz/1 l) cold water

1¾ oz (50 g) bunched fresh dill

2 ribs celery with leaves

4 cloves garlic

2 bay leaves

15 peppercorns

½ teaspoon yellow mustard seeds

MAKES ONE 3-QUART (102-FL OZ/3-L) JAR

Wash the cucumbers thoroughly and soak them in water for 1 hour. Do not cut off the ends—this helps preserve their crunch.

To prepare the brine, in a bowl, dissolve 1 tablespoon salt and the honey in the cold water. Using cold water is crucial to maintain the cucumbers' firm texture.

Place the cucumbers in layers in a large saucepan or bowl, layering them with the dill, celery ribs with leaves, garlic, bay leaves, peppercorns, and mustard seeds. Pour the brine over the cucumbers, making sure they are fully covered. Place a weight on top (such as a plate with a heavy object) to keep them under the liquid. Let stand at room temperature for 2 to 3 days.

After 2 to 3 days, taste the cucumbers, as the fermented flavor will become stronger over time. When you are happy with the result, layer them in a sterilized 3-l jar (see page 241) and pop the jar into the fridge. They can last for several months. The flavor of the cucumbers will continue to develop over time. After about 2 weeks, they will no longer be considered lightly salted but fully fermented pickles.

NOTE

If you can find horseradish or cherry or black currant leaves, I recommend you use it together with the dill and celery ribs. These flavorings are very Ukrainian. Red chiles will also work if you like spicy food.

Lightly Salted Fermented Cucumbers

Ksenia's Fermented Cabbage "Sauerkraut"

Ksenia's Fermented Cabbage "Sauerkraut"

Ksenia is a professional winemaker, the mother of three, and a complete fermentation geek. She'll ferment anything that she can get her hands on, and this recipe is what we call a "classic of the genre." If you've never fermented anything, sauerkraut is a great place to start, as it's both easy to make and has a wonderful flavor. Ksenia is very proud of her Odesan roots and comes from a totally food-obsessed family. Now she teaches her own children to love food in the same way. Every big occasion and major life events are marked by some kind of food. If any guests are invited, the menu revolves around each person's favorite dish and everyone leaves with a doggie bag. Ksenia is a founder of a much-loved bar in the city called Sparkling Wine Gallery, where I used to take many of my foreign guests for a glass of Odesa Black and for a dose of inspiration and true Odesan vitality that Ksenia transmits.

2 lb (1 kg) shredded cabbage
Sea salt
1 small carrot
20 peppercorns
1 bay leaf
Sunflower oil

MAKES ONE 3-CUP (24-FL OZ/700-ML) JAR

Place the cabbage in a large bowl, sprinkle with 1 tablespoon salt, and let stand for about 30 minutes, then squeeze or press the cabbage down so the liquid is released. Tamp the cabbage into a sterilized 3-cup (24–fl oz/700-ml) jar with a lid (see page 241), leaving some space above the tightly packed cabbage because more liquid will be released during this process. Place something heavy on top to press down the cabbage but leave space for air to circulate. Let stand in a warm, dark place for 24 hours; a low temperature stops the fermentation process, which is why the jar with the cabbage needs to be somewhere warm and dark.

After 24 hours, peel and cut the carrot into thin strips and mix it with the cabbage. Add the peppercorns and bay leaf. Press the cabbage down tightly again with the weight. Once a day for 3 to 4 days, remove the weight and poke the cabbage with a wooden spoon or a sushi stick to let the air out. Fermentation time depends on many factors; that's why it's important to taste the cabbage during the process. Once it's ready, store the cabbage in the fridge for up to 1 month. Serve drizzled with sunflower oil.

Sour Eggplant with Onions and Carrots

Tatyana is a chef for whom food is an ultimate expression of love: for people, life, and her beloved Odesa. Vivacious and beautiful, with a sparkly humor, Tatyana prepares food that is just like her. For many years she headed the kitchen of a small, high-end hotel in a historic building, which was famous for serving very seasonal, deeply Odesan food plated with much aplomb and style. She would go to Privoz Market early in the morning to get the best ingredients available. Sometimes Tatyana would buy whole crates of vegetables in season ("too much of a good deal to miss!" she would say) and then make dishes with that ingredient—for the restaurant, friends, passerby—until there was no more. Some great recipes came out of this experimentation, such as this eggplant dish that is tried and tested, going back to an old recipe from south Ukraine. I very much hope that when you visit Odesa (and I hope you will very soon!), you'll get a chance to meet Tatyana and eat her food.

6 eggplants

Sea salt and freshly ground pepper

2 onions

4 large carrots

8 cloves garlic

About ½ cup (4¼ fl oz/125 ml) sunflower oil

A handful of fresh flat-leaf parsley, finely chopped

6 ribs celery with leaves

SERVES 6

Choose young eggplants with thin skin, preferably of the same size. Wash thoroughly, remove the stems, and prick each eggplant several times with a fork.

Bring a large saucepan of water to a boil over high heat and add salt (1 tablespoon per about 1 quart/34 fl oz/1 l water). Add the eggplants to the boiling water, return to a boil, and cook, stirring occasionally, for 5 minutes. They will change color. Transfer the eggplants to a cutting board, cover with another cutting board, and place a weight on top. Let stand for 40 minutes to drain the excess liquid.

Peel and finely chop the onions. Peel and coarsely grate the carrots. Peel and mince the garlic.

Heat the sunflower oil in a large frying pan over medium heat. Add the onions and sauté until golden brown. Add the carrots and fry for 1 minute. Season with salt and pepper. Remove from the heat and let cool. Transfer the onion mixture, including the cooking oil, to a bowl, add the garlic and parsley, and mix.

Squeeze the eggplants to remove any remaining liquid. Make a lengthwise cut in each eggplant, leaving about ¾ inch (2 cm) uncut at the ends. Fill each eggplant with the onion mixture. Tie the stuffed eggplants with the celery ribs. If this is difficult, use kitchen string to tie the eggplants and put the celery ribs between the layers in the container (see below).

In a deep container, place the eggplants tightly in layers. Place a weight on top, e.g., a clean plate with a 3-quart (102–fl oz/3-l) jar of water, to keep them under pressure. Let the eggplants stand at room temperature for 2 to 4 days, depending on the temperature in the room. Fermentation will occur during this time.

Check daily; as soon as liquid appears above the plate, they are ready. The eggplants should acquire a pleasant, mild sourness. Transfer the container to the refrigerator to prevent over-fermentation. The eggplants will keep for up to 3 weeks. Once the eggplants are fermented, they are ready to be served as an appetizer. Cut them into portion-size pieces. If you like, drizzle with sunflower oil and sprinkle with minced garlic.

PREMIUM BANANAS

Sour Eggplant with Onions and Carrots

Spicy Pickled Plums

Spicy Pickled Plums

At one point 10 percent of Odesa's population were Italians, who had come here during the wheat boom to make their fortunes and to enjoy the climate. At the time, many Italian theater and opera companies were touring in and around Odesa. The melody of the classic Neapolitan song "O sole mio!" was written by the composer Eduardo di Capua, while he was staying in Odesa, a city he came to love. There were also lots of factories making *makarony* (a word we use to mean all kinds of pasta), which was dried in the sun, just as it was made in Naples. Even now, there is a significant Italian diaspora, people who came in the 1990s and happily settled down, managing hotels and restaurants and working as coffee roasters. Many are from Genoa; they say that they like how the two cities feel similar.

This recipe comes from my husband's Aunt Tanya. She was married to Pavel Rovazzo, who came from an Italian dynasty, while Tanya's ancestors were of Greek origin. When she and Pavel met in the 1960s in Soviet Odesa, they quickly fell in love. Both came from families who loved to eat and spent lots of time cooking and enjoying huge feasts. Everything was prepared from scratch, as anything shop-bought was deemed inferior. Like this amazing recipe for pickled plums. Tanya could easily get these plums from the shop or the market, but she always made them herself.

About 2¼ cups (17 fl oz/500 ml) water

10½ oz (300 g) sugar

⅓ cup (2¾ fl oz/80 ml) cider vinegar

About 3½ tablespoons (50 ml) cognac

7 bay leaves

10 whole cloves

10 allspice berries

10 peppercorns

18 oz (500 g) unripe plums, left whole

MAKE ONE 3-CUP (24-FL OZ/700-ML) JAR

Pour the water into a saucepan and add the sugar, vinegar, cognac, bay leaves, cloves, allspice berries, and peppercorns. Stir and bring the brine to a boil over high heat, then boil for 10 minutes.

Place the plums in a bowl and pour the hot brine over them. Let stand for 1 hour. Drain the brine back into the saucepan, then bring it to a boil and pour over the plums again. Let stand for 1 hour. Repeat the process again and let stand for 1 hour.

Transfer the plums and the brine, including all the spices, to a sterilized 3-cup (24-fl oz/700-ml) jar (see page 241), close the lid, and refrigerate. The plums will be ready in 10 to 12 hours and will keep in the fridge for up to 3 months.

Mulberry Jam

Everyone who grew up in Odesa will tell you their childhood stories about climbing mulberry trees, munching on these delicate berries and ruining many a T-shirt in the process—black mulberries stain everything they come in contact with! The mulberry trees—and fruit trees in general—are everywhere in the city, growing wild on the streets and in private gardens, even in neighborhoods full of high-rise buildings. These new districts were built around the trees. This recipe belongs to Vadim, now a famous Odesan chef who uses his childhood memories to create recipes. He fondly remembers bringing lots of freshly picked mulberries home for his mom to prepare this amazing summer jam, which she still makes every year. Vadim remembers feeling such a sense of achievement when he could "procure" food for the family!

3¼ lb (1.5 kg) mulberries

3¼ lb (1 .5 kg)
superfine (caster) sugar

MAKES FOUR
1⅓-CUP (11-FL OZ/330-ML)
JARS

In a large bowl, layer the sugar and mulberries alternately, starting with a layer of sugar, then a single layer of mulberries; repeat a couple more times. Let the mixture stand for 1 to 1½ hours so the berries release their juice.

Transfer the mulberries with their juice into a large saucepan. Slowly bring to a boil over medium heat; this should take 20 to 25 minutes. Once it starts boiling, simmer for 5 minutes, stirring gently and scraping the bottom of the pan with a wooden spatula. Using a spoon, skim off any foam that forms on the surface.

Let the jam cool, then transfer into four 1⅓ cup (11-fl oz/330-ml) sterilized jars with lids (see page 241), distributing the berries and syrup evenly up to the very top. Close the lids tightly and turn the jars upside down so they are resting on the lids. Let them cool completely in this position. Store the jam in the fridge for up to 1 month.

NOTE

When making the jam in Odesa, we use a nonreactive pan with a flat bottom. The size depends on the amount of jam; typically the pan is 12 to 20 inches (30 to 50 cm) in diameter and with low sides (4 to 6 inches/10 to 15 cm).

Mulberry Jam

Rose Petal Jam

Rose Petal Jam

The fact that food can also be a medicine is an important part of Odesa's culinary story. There are food market stalls that sell all sorts of herbs and potions. The women (they are always women) who sell these concoctions will be very happy to suggest what you should (and shouldn't!) eat to treat this or that ailment. Eating for health is a normal part of Odesa's culinary lexicon. This recipe is as pretty and delicious as it is potent. Generations of Odesan children grew up being fed spoonfuls of this jam at the merest sign of a sore throat. The recipe belongs to Katerina, the daughter of a sea captain, who now works as a sea navigator. She and her mother usually collect lots of roses in bloom to make this jam. If you prepare it, be sure to use roses that haven't been sprayed with chemicals. Try to use tea roses, which have a sweet, delicate flavor.

10½ oz (300 g) rose petals

30 oz (850 g)
superfine (caster) sugar, divided

1 teaspoon (5 g) citric acid

About 1 cup

7 fl oz (200 ml) water

MAKES THREE
1¼-CUP (10–FL OZ/300-ML)
JARS

In a large bowl, mix the rose petals, 10½ oz (300 g) of the sugar, and the citric acid. Let stand for 1 hour to macerate.

In a large saucepan, combine the water and the remaining 19½ oz (550 g) sugar. Slowly bring to a boil over medium-high heat, stirring until the sugar is completely dissolved. Add the rose petal mixture to the boiling syrup, reduce the heat, and simmer for 15 to 20 minutes.

Transfer the jam into 3 warm 1¼-cup (10–fl oz/300-ml) sterilized jars with lids (see page 241), close the lids, and let them cool. Store the jam in the fridge for up to 3 months.

Yellow Cherry Jam

Yellow cherries have a very short season; once picked, they must be eaten or preserved quickly as they will darken. Husband and wife Kostya and Lyuda have a tradition of making this jam every year for their family and friends. I am a lucky recipient of one precious jar each year, but their daughter Katya gets the lion's share. Like most teenagers these days, Katya prefers to eat "cooler" things that aren't made at home, but this jam is something she really loves, slathering golden spoonfuls on toast with butter or eating it straight from the jar. Her parents are only too happy, especially since in Odesa's culture anything made with yellow cherries is thought to have medicinal properties. This jam, for instance, is particularly good for children's immune systems.

2 lb (1 kg) yellow cherries, such as Rainier

1¾ lb (800 g) superfine (caster) sugar

½ lemon

Seeds of 1 vanilla bean or 1 teaspoon vanilla paste

MAKES TWO 2¼-CUP (17-FL OZ/500-ML) JARS

Remove the pits from the cherries, trying to keep the shape of the cherries intact. Place the cherries in a large saucepan, sprinkle with the sugar, and stir gently to coat. Refrigerate overnight.

Place the saucepan with the cherries over high heat and bring to a boil, stirring gently with a wooden spatula, then reduce the heat and simmer for 5 minutes, skimming off the foam. Let the jam stand at room temperature for 8 to 10 hours.

Cut the lemon crosswise into slices, then cut each slice into 4 pieces. Add to the cherries and bring to a boil again, and simmer for 5 minutes. Let stand at room temperature again for 8 to 10 hours.

Add the vanilla and bring the jam to a boil for a third time, then simmer for 5 minutes.

Once the jam has cooled, transfer it into two 2¼-cup (17-fl oz/500-ml) sterilized jars with lids (see page 241), close the lids, and store the jam in the fridge for up to 1 month.

Yellow Cherry Jam

Apricot Jam with Apricot Kernels

Apricot Kompot

Apricot Jam with Apricot Kernels

We began our cooking session with Olya by going to a flea market. Her late mother always made apricot jam in a huge brass basin, which has long since gone missing. Olya was determined to replicate the process of making her mum's recipe down to the last detail and, luckily, we found exactly the right pot. Cooking and then canning apricots is still a popular pastime in Ukraine. In and around Odesa, people prepare this recipe with the kernels of apricot pits, which give the jam a better texture and make it more nutritious. This is a recipe that shows beautifully the frugality of the Odesans and our willingness to go to great lengths to use every bit of an ingredient. If you haven't "suffered" enough for a dish, you haven't put in enough love!

4½ lb (2 kg) ripe apricots

2 lb (1 kg) plus 3½ oz (100 g) superfine (caster) sugar, divided

Boiling water as needed

½ cup (4 oz/150 ml)

MAKES FOUR 2¼-CUP (17–FL OZ/500-ML) JARS

Be sure to choose ripe apricots for the jam. Cut each apricot in half lengthwise and remove the pit; reserve the pits. Place the apricots in a large saucepan, sprinkle with the 2 lb (1 kg) sugar, and stir gently to coat. Refrigerate for at least 10 hours or up to overnight.

Let the apricot pits dry, then crack open the pits and remove the kernels inside. Put the kernels in a bowl, pour boiling water over them, and let stand for 1 to 2 hours. Drain the kernels and rub off the skins. Set aside.

Place the saucepan with the apricots over medium-high heat and bring to a boil, then reduce the heat and simmer for 10 minutes. Let stand at room temperature for at least 10 hours or up to overnight. Gently move the jam around by sliding a wooden spatula along the edges of the pan.

Bring the apricots to a boil again and simmer for 10 minutes. Let stand at room temperature again for 10 to 12 hours.

In another saucepan, combine the remaining 3½ oz (100 g) sugar and the water and bring to a boil over high heat. Add the apricot kernels and boil for 15 minutes. Drain the kernels.

Bring the jam to a boil for a third time, add the apricot kernels, reduce the heat to low, and simmer for 10 minutes. Remove from the heat and let the jam cool.

Transfer the jam into four 2¼-cup (17–fl oz/500-ml) sterilized jars with lids (see page 241), close the lids, and store the jam in the fridge for up to 1 month.

Apricot Kompot on Ice

"Olechka, drink the *kompot*! It's not *just kompot*, it's a glass of pure health!" Olya laughs as she remembers her grandmother's instructions. Olya grew up in Kazakhstan but spent all her summers in Odesa being looked after—and fed—by her typical Odesan granny. So many of our grandmothers have a sole purpose in life: to cook a myriad of dishes for their grandchildren every day. It's the way they can show love, care, and even their slight obsession with seeing the children growing happily plump during the summer.

"You couldn't see my ears behind my cheeks!" says Olya, but looking at her now, a beautiful, petite woman, it's difficult to imagine that she was ever a chubby little girl!

When they weren't busy eating, she and her grandma would go to the market to choose ingredients, visit the theater, and go to the beach, exploring the city as if they were characters in a fairy tale, wandering through a magical land.

Now Olya lives in her grandma's flat in Odesa—a place where her grandmother's spirit lives on. In every object, you can almost feel the love passed on from one generation to the next.

2 lb (1 kg) ripe apricots

5¼ oz (150 g) superfine (caster) sugar or 3½ oz (100 g) honey

About 2 quarts (68 fl oz/2 l) cold water

Ice cubes

MAKES ½ CUPS (52 FL OZ/1.5 L)

Cut each apricot in half lengthwise and remove the pit. Place the apricots in a large saucepan, add the sugar, and cover with the cold water. Bring to a boil over high heat, then reduce the heat and simmer for 5 minutes. Chill in the fridge and serve in jars or glasses over ice.

HOW TO STERILIZE JARS AND LIDS

A number of recipes in this chapter call for sterilizing jars and lids before adding jam or other preserves. This is an important safety step that kills bacteria and yeasts, which can cause your jam to spoil and ruin the fruits of your labor. Sterilizing is really quite easy to do.

First, wash the jars in warm soapy water and rinse thoroughly. Place the jars and their lids in a pot of boiling water (make sure they are covered with the water) or over steam for 10 minutes. Then put the sterilized jars upside down on a clean towel to drain completely.

Kompot with Ripe Strawberries

Kompot with Ripe Strawberries

In Ukraine a *kompot* is a fruit-based drink that is especially enjoyed by children. Here's a really simple recipe from Oksana, who ran the city's tourist office before the war. As she proudly says about herself: "I made the city's guests fall in love with Odesa." Now Oksana dreams of making Odesa a popular destination 365 days a year and puts all her energy into promoting Odesa throughout Ukraine and beyond. Her recipe for *kompot* relies on ripe, sweet strawberries in season, which make the drink truly special.

2 lb (1 kg) strawberries

About 2 quarts (68 fl oz/2 l) water

4½ oz (130 g) superfine (caster) sugar

Juice of 1 lemon

Ice cubes for serving

MAKES ABOUT 2 QUARTS (68 FL OZ/2 L)

Remove the stems from the strawberries. Pour the water into a large saucepan, add the sugar, and cover with a lid. Bring to a boil over medium heat.

When the water is boiling, add the strawberries and return to a boil, then reduce the heat to a gentle simmer. Cover and cook for 5 minutes, then remove from the heat.

While the *kompot* is still hot, transfer it to a pitcher together with the strawberries and let cool, then add the lemon juice. Refrigerate until chilled. Serve the strawberries in the *kompot*, along with the liquid, in jars or glasses over ice.

NOTE

If you add the strawberries to boiling sweet water and cook them briefly, they will hold their shape and the kompot *will remain beautifully clear. The strawberries from the* kompot *are perfectly edible—nothing goes to waste in Odesa!*

Sweet Things

CAKES, DESSERTS, AND PASTRY

Meringue Cookies "Rozochki"

Meringue Cookies "Rozochki"

No matter how many of these golden "roses" you bake, with their tender and fragile meringue, there will never be enough! One of my oldest and dearest friends is Nastya, whom I've known for almost forty years. We both have a vivid memory from our childhood—the day we "attacked" a huge plate of these cookies, freshly baked by her mother. We couldn't stop until we had polished off the last crumb. That evening, back with the rest of the family, we got scolded by Nastya's mother for leaving the grown-ups without any dessert. How could we have known that adults loved sweets just as much as we did?

11½ oz (325 g) all-purpose flour, plus more for dusting

9 oz (250 g) cold unsalted butter

9 oz (250 g) curd cheese (see page 28)

3 egg yolks

2 cold egg whites

4¼ oz (120 g) superfine (caster) sugar

MAKES 30

Sift the flour into a large bowl. Coarsely grate the butter into the bowl. Rub the flour and butter together until the mixture resembles breadcrumbs. In a medium bowl, mix together the curd cheese and egg yolks until smooth. Transfer the cheese mixture to the bowl with the flour mixture and stir to combine. Bring together into a soft dough, wrap in plastic wrap, and refrigerate for 1 hour.

Preheat the oven to 350°F (180°C). Line a baking sheet with parchment paper.

In a large bowl, using a stand mixer on medium-high speed or a hand mixer on high, whisk the egg whites until foamy, then gradually add the sugar. Continue whisking until soft peaks form. The whites should still be soft and shiny, not whipped into a dense foam. Set aside.

Generously sprinkle a work surface with flour. Divide the dough into 2 equal pieces. Return one piece to the refrigerator. Roll out the other dough piece into a rectangle about 1⁄16 inch (4 mm) thick. Using a spoon or a silicone spatula, cover the entire surface of the dough with half of the whipped egg whites in an even layer, leaving ¾ inch (2 cm) at the edge nearest you uncovered. Starting from the side farthest from you, roll the dough tightly into a spiral. Using a sharp knife, cut the dough into ¾-inch (2-cm) slices. Place the cookies on the prepared baking sheet, spacing them ¾ to 1¼ inches (2 to 3 cm) apart.

Bake for 20 to 25 minutes, or until golden brown. Transfer the baking sheet to a wire rack and let the cookies cool, then transfer them directly to the rack. Repeat with the remaining dough.

Apple "Vertuta" Pastry

Apple "Vertuta" Pastry

Larisa is a ceramics artist who became well-known in the city during the Covid pandemic when she started creating personalized mugs with witty, wise, and inspiring inscriptions. We spent a beautiful day with Larisa in her studio, known as her "laboratory of beauty," recreating a recipe from her grandmother, which was lost when Larisa was four. When you bake this pastry, a pool of sugar and butter will inevitably escape from underneath the pie, creating the most delicious caramel. When I was a child, my grandmother also made a version of *vertuta* using a Soviet-era pot aptly called *chudo* (wonder). Many Odesan families, including ours, didn't have an oven at home, and so this wondrous pot allowed us to use the stove like an oven. Both Larisa and I have fond childhood memories of fighting with our families over who would get *chudo*'s caramel!

1 egg

About 4¾ tablespoons (2¼ fl oz/70 ml) sunflower oil

About 4¾ tablespoons (2¼ fl oz/70 ml) very warm water

10½ oz (300 g) all-purpose flour, plus more for dusting

Sea salt

1 teaspoon baking soda

18 oz (500 g) apples

7 oz (200 g) superfine (caster) sugar

1¾ oz (50 g) unsalted butter

Sunflower oil (if frying the *vertuta*) or 1 medium egg beaten with 1 tablespoon whole milk (if baking the *vertuta*)

1¾ oz (50 g) confectioners' sugar

MAKES 1 LARGE OR 6 SMALL *VERTUTAS*

In a small bowl, whisk egg, sunflower oil, and warm water until smooth. In a large bowl, combine flour, 1.5 teaspoons salt, and baking soda. Pour in the egg mixture and mix until a dough forms. Transfer to a work surface and knead until smooth and elastic; avoid adding extra flour. Cover with an overturned bowl and let rest 30 to 40 minutes.

Meanwhile, grate or finely dice apples and drain in a fine-mesh sieve. Lightly flour the work surface. Roll dough into a 0.08-inch (2 mm) thick circle. Spread apples evenly in a thin layer, then sprinkle with superfine sugar and dot with small butter pieces. Carefully roll the dough from one side, ensuring filling stays inside. Seal ends and seam tightly. Gently stretch the roll on both sides, then twist along its length (as if wringing laundry). Finally, coil into a spiral or snail shape. Fry or bake as desired.

To fry the *vertuta*, pour sunflower oil into a large frying pan to a depth of ⅜ inch (1 cm) and heat over medium heat until hot. Carefully place the *vertuta* in the pan and reduce the heat to low. Cover with a lid and fry for 20 minutes on each side, or until golden brown.

To bake the *vertuta*, reheat the oven to 350°F (180°C). Line a baking sheet with parchment paper and carefully place the *vertuta* on it. Brush the *vertuta* with the beaten egg mixture. Bake for about 40 minutes, or until golden brown.

Sprinkle the fried or baked *vertuta* with confectioners' sugar and serve.

NOTE

To make smaller vertutas (easier for beginners), divide dough into 6 equal pieces and assemble as directed. If frying, immediately place each rolled vertuta in the pan to preserve juiciness and crispiness. For variations, substitute apples with pears or grated pumpkin. For savory vertutas, use fillings like stewed cabbage or cottage cheese with dill; omit superfine sugar, confectioners' sugar, and butter.

Baked Curd Cheesecake "Zapekanka"

Viktorija is a founder of a school of etiquette where she offers a unique mix of teaching, combining style with culture, history, and Ukrainian traditions. For Viktorija, beauty doesn't need to cost a lot and is just as much about what happens on the inside as well as on the outside. It was wonderful spending time with her, recording her recipe while surrounded by gorgeous plates, cutlery, furniture, and Viktorija's radiant, soulful personality.

3½ oz (100 g) golden raisins

Boiling water as needed

1¾ oz (50 g) unsalted butter, plus more for greasing

10 eggs

Sea salt

2 lb (1 kg) curd cheese (see page 28)

Zest of 1 small orange

Seeds from 1 vanilla bean or 1 teaspoon vanilla paste

3 tablespoons semolina flour, divided

7 oz (200 g) sugar

SERVES 8–10

Preheat the oven to 350°F (180°C).

In a small bowl, pour boiling water over the raisins to plump them up, then drain in a fine-mesh sieve.

Line a plate with paper towels. Melt the butter in a small frying pan over medium heat. Add the raisins and cook, stirring constantly, for 7 to 10 minutes, or until they are fully soaked with the butter. Transfer the raisins to the paper towel–lined plate to absorb any excess butter.

Separate the egg yolks from the whites; set the whites aside. In a medium bowl, using a stand mixer on medium-high speed or a hand mixer on high, mix together the yolks and 1 teaspoon salt until smooth. In a large bowl, rub the curd cheese through a fine-mesh sieve or blend it with a stick blender until smooth. Then add the yolks and mix thoroughly until combined. Add the orange zest, vanilla, and 2 tablespoons of the semolina flour and mix again to distribute the ingredients evenly. Add the raisins and mix well.

In a medium bowl, beat together the egg whites and sugar until stiff peaks form. Using a silicone spatula, gradually fold the whites into the yolk mixture, adding them in portions.

Grease a 10¼-inch (26-cm) baking pan with butter and sprinkle the bottom of the pan with the remaining 1 tablespoon semolina flour; alternatively, use a silicone mold. Transfer the cheesecake mixture to the prepared pan.

Bake for 40 to 50 minutes, or until deep golden brown. Transfer the pan to a wire rack and let cool completely, then carefully turn the cheesecake out of the pan.

NOTE

To make the egg yolks even more vibrant, sprinkle them with salt in advance and let stand for 7 to 10 minutes. Their color will intensify, and the zapekanka will turn out even more golden. Every Odesan grandmother does this if she hasn't managed to buy farm-fresh eggs at Privoz Market.

Baked Curd Cheesecake "Zapekanka"

Limor's Cookies with Poppy Seeds

Limor's Cookies with Poppy Seeds

Limor's great-grandparents came to Israel from Odesa before the Communist Revolution with wonderful memories about their city of origin. Her great-grandfather, who became a well-known artist in Israel, had originally graduated from the Odesan Art School. He reminisces fondly about one café in the center of Odesa, called Fanconi, where artists and local intelligentsia would gather. The glamorous café was founded by two Italian brothers, and Fanconi is still there. Even though it lost many of its original features, a lot of old photographs still exist that convey the spirit of the original place and Odesa as it was a century ago.

After Limor's great-grandparents moved to Israel, their daughter, Limor's grandmother, moved to live in a kibbutz. (A kibbutz is a social community where all meals are taken communally in a large dining hall.) She used to go to the big kitchens of the dining hall to make cookies for her family. This old Jewish cookie recipe belongs to that era. Limor still remembers her grandmother bringing big tins filled with these cookies whenever she visited her and her family in Tel Aviv. Her grandmother didn't leave a written recipe, but Limor, who's now a chef, has managed to recreate the recipe quite close to the original. Having never visited Odesa, Limor is hoping to visit soon the city of her origins.

5¼ oz (150 g) unsalted butter

3 oz (90 g) plus 2 tablespoons light brown sugar, divided

Zest of ⅓ orange

3 tablespoons fresh orange juice

2 tablespoons sunflower oil

Seeds from 1 vanilla bean or 1 teaspoon vanilla paste

1 egg

10½ oz (300 g) all-purpose flour

1 teaspoon baking powder

1 tablespoon poppy seeds

MAKES 40

In a large bowl, beat the butter and the 3 oz (90 g) brown sugar with an electric mixer on medium speed until light and fluffy. Add the orange zest and juice, sunflower oil, vanilla, and egg and beat again until well combined.

In a small bowl, stir together the flour and baking powder. Add the flour to the butter mixture and beat until combined, then add the poppy seeds and beat until combined. Cover with plastic wrap and refrigerate for at least 1 hour.

Preheat the oven to 325°F (160°C). Line a large baking sheet with parchment paper.

Divide the dough in half and roll one half with your hands into a cylinder shape about 2 inches (5 cm) wide. Sprinkle the 2 tablespoons brown sugar on another baking sheet and roll the dough cylinder in the sugar to coat evenly. Using a sharp knife, cut the dough into slices about ¼ inch (5 mm) thick. Transfer to the parchment-lined baking sheet, leaving some space between the cookies. Repeat with the remaining dough.

Bake the cookies for 20 to 25 minutes, or until golden brown all over. Let them cool for a few minutes and then enjoy right away, or store in an airtight container at room temperature.

Ukrainian Fried Dough "Khrustiky"

Alena is a writer who has worked in the Odesa Literary Museum all her life, devoting her career to researching and writing about her beloved Odesa. Alena has Ukrainian and Greek roots, which might explain why she has this tranquil, almost majestic way of carrying herself in the world, like a statue of a Greek goddess. She brings that same serenity to her cooking, which makes everyone want to gather around to hear her stories and eat her food.

Alena's love for cooking was inspired by her Aunt Marusya, who was famous for her food. Marusya was even asked to cook for weddings and large gatherings in neighboring villages. Alena chose this recipe for the book because it perfectly represents how she sees the Odesan approach to food: a simple Ukrainian dish made extra special by how it looks. These little fried "crispies" (*khrust* is the crunching sound that a twig might make when it's broken) are prepared everywhere in Ukraine, but the use of this old, home-manufactured knife inherited from Marusya to slice through the dough is Alena's touch. The little wheel creates a delicate ridged effect. The fried ribbons go so well with a cup of coffee, or they can be hung on a Christmas tree as edible decorations!

2 eggs

2 tablespoons superfine (caster) sugar

Sea salt

Seeds from 1 vanilla bean or 1 teaspoon vanilla paste

Zest of 1 lemon

2 tablespoons vodka

7 oz (200 g) all-purpose flour

Sunflower oil for frying

1¾ oz (50 g) confectioners' sugar

MAKES 40 PASTRIES

In a large bowl, beat the eggs, superfine sugar, and ¼ teaspoon salt until well combined. Add the vanilla, lemon zest, and vodka and mix thoroughly. Gradually incorporate the flour while stirring continuously. Knead the dough well until smooth.

Divide the dough into 4 equal pieces and knead each piece into a ball. Cover with plastic wrap and refrigerate for 20 to 30 minutes.

Roll out each ball of dough as thinly as possible; the thinner the dough, the tastier these will be. Cut the rolled dough into strips, then cut each strip into diamond shapes. Make a small slit in the center of each diamond and pass one corner through the slit to create a twisted shape.

Line a plate with paper towels. Heat sunflower oil in a large frying pan or a deep cauldron over medium heat. Working in batches as needed, drop the twisted diamonds into the hot oil; they should float and begin to brown slightly. Fry for about 30 seconds, then turn them over and fry the other side until light golden. Using a slotted spoon, transfer the pastries to the paper towel-lined plate to absorb any excess oil. While they are still warm, sprinkle generously with confectioners' sugar.

Ukrainian Fried Dough "Khrustiky"

дача
ресторан
БУЛЬВАР
85

Challah Bread with a Blessing

Challah Bread with a Blessing

Challah is perhaps the quintessential Jewish bread. Lena, a writer, musician, and mother of three, has lived in Paris for many years and still makes this bread regularly. There's a lot of meaning in how challah is shaped and baked, following a ritual steeped in ancient traditions. Lena says that when kneading the dough, you must make a *bracha*, a blessing in Hebrew. All three children helped Lena prepare the bread for this book, each of them sending a wish for its success. Thank you so much, dear friends.

2½ lb (1.15 kg)
all-purpose flour, divided

About 1 teaspoon (¾ oz/24 g)
instant dry yeast

About 1½ cups
(12½ fl oz/375 ml) warm water

5 eggs

3 egg yolks

6½ oz (120 g)
superfine (caster) sugar

About ½ cup (4¼ fl oz/125 ml)
sunflower oil

Sea salt

EGG WASH

1 medium egg yolk

2 tablespoons whole milk

MAKES 1 LOAF

In a large bowl of a stand mixer, using the dough hook, on low speed mix together 8 oz (225 g) of the flour, the yeast, and warm water. Let stand until foamy. Add the remaining flour, the eggs and egg yolks, sugar, sunflower oil, and 1 teaspoon salt to the yeast mixture and knead the dough until smooth and elastic. Transfer the dough to a clean bowl, cover with plastic wrap, and let rise in a warm place for about 2 hours, or until it has at least doubled in size.

Line a baking sheet with parchment paper. Divide the dough into 4 equal pieces. Roll each piece into a rope 8 to 10 inches (20 to 25 cm) long. Braid 4 of the ropes together to shape a challah. Transfer the challah to the prepared baking sheet and cover with plastic wrap. Let rise in a warm place for about 1½ hours, or until doubled in size.

Preheat the oven to 350°F (180°C).

To make the egg wash, in a small bowl, whisk together the egg yolk and milk. Brush the challah twice with the egg wash. Bake the challahs for 30 to 40 minutes, or until golden brown. Transfer the challahs to a wire rack and let cool.

Mazurka Cookies

You might remember the iconic scene in Sergei Eisenstein's cult black-and-white 1925 film, *Battleship Potemkin*, when a baby in a carriage slowly tumbles down a long, steep flight of steps. Alyona's great-grandfather, who lost both of his legs during the First World War, starred in that scene as a young boy and became a bit of a legend in Odesa as a result. A working actor with such a disability in those days was certainly a rarity. Many years later, his great-granddaughter, Alena's daughter, would follow in his acting footsteps and studied film in London, where her teachers were astounded to discover that she had such a close connection to that era-defining film.

Alyona chose her mum's cookie recipe because it reminded her so much of her carefree time in childhood spent in their *dvorik* courtyard.

- 7 oz (200 g) walnut halves
- 7 oz (200 g) raisins
- 7 oz (200 g) firmly packed golden brown sugar
- 1 large egg
- 3½ oz (100 g) unsalted butter, melted and cooled slightly
- 7 oz (200 g) all-purpose flour
- ½ teaspoon baking soda
- 1 tablespoon fresh lemon juice

MAKES 25–30

Preheat the oven to 350°F (180°C). Line a baking sheet with parchment paper.

Finely chop the walnuts and raisins and set aside. In a large bowl, whisk together the brown sugar and egg until just combined. Add the melted butter, then add the flour and baking soda and mix well. Add the walnuts, raisins, and lemon juice and mix by hand. Transfer the mixture to the prepared baking sheet and smooth it into an even layer about ⅜ inch (1 cm) thick.

Bake for 20 to 25 minutes, or until golden brown. Transfer the baked cookie, still on the parchment paper, to a wire rack to cool. While it's still slightly warm and sticky, cut into rhombus shapes with sides 1¼ to 1½ inches (3 to 4 cm) long and let cool completely.

Mazurka Cookies

Poppy Seed Roll

Poppy Seed Roll

Mykola and I have collaborated on many projects over the years. An incredible baker, he has a rare talent for teaching his craft. His passion for sourdough and baking is infectious. He teaches the technicality, but more importantly, he conveys why sourdough baking is worth the effort: the reasons are nutritional, social, and even spiritual. In 2022, Mykola and I founded Bake for Ukraine, which, to this day, feeds people in Ukraine and promotes our traditional bread-making techniques.

This recipe for a poppy seed roll is a classic in Ukrainian cuisine from Mykola's future cookbook.

DOUGH

3½ oz (100 g) stiff starter (Lievito Madre at its peak)

9 oz (250 g) whole wheat flour

About 6 tablespoons (3 fl oz/100 ml) whole milk

1 medium egg

1¾ oz (45 g) superfine (caster) sugar

1 teaspoons salt

1¾ oz (50 g) unsalted butter

FILLING

12 oz (340 g) poppy seeds

6 oz (170 g) superfine (caster) sugar

About ¾ cup plus 2 tablespoons (7½ fl oz/225 ml) whole milk

4 tablespoons (55 g)

unsalted butter

1 large egg white

Seeds from 1 vanilla bean or 1 teaspoon vanilla paste

1 egg yolk beaten with 2 tablespoons whole milk

SYRUP

2 tablespoons water

2 tablespoons cognac or rum

1 oz (30 g) superfine

(caster) sugar

MAKES 1 ROLL

To prepare the dough, in a food processor fitted with the dough hook attachment, combine the stiff starter, flour, milk, and egg. Knead on speed 2 for about 7 minutes, or until smooth. Cover the food processor bowl with a kitchen towel and let the dough rest for 45 minutes. Add the sugar and knead until incorporated. Add the salt and then the butter in two additions, kneading for about 10 minutes, or until smooth and uniform. Transfer the dough to a greased bowl, cover with plastic wrap, and let rise in a warm place (about 75°F/24°C) for 4 to 5 hours, or until doubled in size.

Meanwhile, prepare the filling: Working in batches, use a clean coffee grinder or a spice grinder to grind the poppy seeds. Blend the ground poppy seeds, sugar, and milk until smooth. Transfer the mixture to a frying pan, add the butter, and heat gently over medium-low heat until the butter melts, stirring constantly so the mixture doesn't stick. Let cool, then add the egg white and vanilla and mix well.

Line a baking sheet with parchment paper. Knead the risen dough lightly, then let it rest under plastic wrap for 10 minutes. Roll out the dough into a rectangle 16 by 10 inches (40 by 25 cm). Spread the poppy seed filling evenly over the dough, leaving a about a ¼-inch (5-mm) border uncovered. Starting with a long side, roll the dough into a tight spiral. Place the rolled-up dough on the prepared baking sheet and cover with plastic wrap. Proof in the refrigerator for about 10 hours or at room temperature for 3 to 4 hours, or until the dough is soft and risen. Brush the roll twice with the beaten egg yolk mixture.

Preheat the oven to 375°F (190°C).

Bake the roll for 35 to 40 minutes, or until golden brown.

Meanwhile, prepare the syrup: In a small saucepan, combine the water, cognac, and sugar. Set over low heat and bring the mixture to a boil, stirring occasionally. Cook until the sugar dissolves completely and the syrup begins to thicken a little. Remove from the heat and let cool.

Transfer the baked roll to a wire rack and brush with the warm syrup. Let the roll cool completely before slicing.

Odesa Black's "Drunken" Prunes with Walnuts

Alina comes from a well-known family of local winemakers. Their vineyard, Villa Tinta, has a shop in the city where visitors can sample wine as well as these prunes, which they soak in a dry red wine called Odesa Black. This is an amazing indigenous wine variety, which I hope will soon be available for people to try all over the world. In Odesa we normally serve these prunes at the beginning of a meal, but they also make a great dessert.

10½ oz (300 g) prunes

About 1 cup (9 fl oz/250 ml) boiling water

3½ oz (100 g) walnut halves

1¼ cups (10 fl oz/300 ml) dry red wine, such as Odesa Black

3 tablespoons honey

About ⅔ cup (5 fl oz/150 ml) heavy cream

2 tablespoons (15 g) confectioners' sugar

SERVES 4–6

Remove the pits from the prunes, keeping the prunes whole. In a bowl, pour the boiling water over the prunes. Let stand for 20 minutes so the prunes will become softer and easier to stuff. Drain well.

Cut each walnut half in half again. Lightly toast the walnuts in a frying pan over medium-high heat. Stuff each prune with a walnut piece.

Put the stuffed prunes in a nonstick or heavy-bottomed saucepan, pour in the wine, and let soak at room temperature for 2 hours. Add the honey and bring to a boil over medium-high heat, then reduce the heat to low and simmer the prunes for 1½ to 2 hours. A lot of the wine will evaporate as it simmers; you will pour the wine that remains in the pan over the prunes when serving. Remove from the heat and let the prunes cool.

Using a whisk, mix the cream with the confectioners' sugar just until the sugar dissolves, then refrigerate to cool for a while. When the prunes are cool, transfer them to a deep bowl, pour in the remaining wine from the pan, and cover with the whipped cream.

Odesa Black's "Drunken" Prunes with Walnuts

bistrot

Napoleon Cake

Napoleon Cake

The Napoleon is a cake found in many parts of Eastern Europe; it's a sibling of the French mille-feuille, or a cake of a "thousand layers." This version is special to Odesa: It's light and very moist. The recipe comes from Maxim's grandmother, who would prepare this huge, delicious cake in her tiny kitchen with its standard Soviet oven. Maxim explains that for many years, he couldn't understand how his granny could manage to make such a big cake. The secret was in the way she put together each sheet of pastry, like overlapping flower petals. This recipe makes a smaller cake but one that's just as exquisite. Maxim is a well-known restaurateur who's managed to open many successful restaurants in Odesa, including the French bistro Lou Lou. Each of them pays tribute to the culture and sensibilities of Odesa and its people.

DOUGH

21 oz (600 g) all-purpose flour, plus more as needed

7 oz (200 g) ice-cold unsalted butter

7 oz (200 g) sour cream

1½ teaspoons cider vinegar

About ⅔ cup (5 fl oz/150 ml) ice-cold water

CREAM

7 egg yolks

7 tablespoons all-purpose flour

Sea salt

About 5¾ cups (46 fl oz/1.35 l) warm water

21 oz (600 g) sweetened condensed milk

4 tablespoons superfine (caster) sugar

Seeds from 1 vanilla bean or 1 teaspoon vanilla paste

1 lb (450 g) unsalted butter, at room temperature

1 cup (100 g) walnut halves

SERVES 10

To prepare the dough, sift the flour into a large bowl and coarsely grate the ice-cold butter into it. Rub the flour and butter together with your fingertips until the mixture resembles breadcrumbs. Add the sour cream, vinegar, and ice-cold water, then knead the dough by hand (not in a stand mixer) until it is soft and no longer sticky. If it sticks to your hands, add a little more flour. Dust a work surface with flour and divide the dough into 8 equal pieces. Wrap separately in plastic wrap and refrigerate for 2 to 3 hours.

To prepare the cream, in a medium bowl, mix the egg yolks with the flour and a pinch of salt until smooth; it's easier to do this with your hands. In a large saucepan, combine the warm water, condensed milk, and sugar and heat over medium-high heat, stirring until the sugar is completely dissolved. Slowly pour 1¼ cups (10 fl oz/300 ml) of the milk mixture into the yolk mixture, stirring constantly to prevent lumps.

Set the saucepan with the remaining milk mixture over low heat and warm it to about 104°F (40°C). Gradually pour the yolk mixture into the pan while stirring vigorously. Cook the cream over low heat, stirring constantly, until it thickens to the consistency of thick sour cream. Remove from the heat and let cool for 1 to 2 hours. Once the cream has cooled but is still slightly warm, add the vanilla. While stirring, gradually add the soft butter in small pieces until the cream is silky and smooth. Let cool completely.

Preheat the oven to 350°F (180°C).

Generously dust a work surface with flour and roll out each piece of dough into a circle. Keep turning the dough while you are rolling it out to prevent sticking. Transfer the dough to a sheet of parchment paper, then continue rolling until it reaches a thickness of 1⁄16 to 1⁄8 inch (2 to 3 mm) and is slightly larger than your springform pan. Make sure the edges are thinner than the middle. Transfer the disk, still on the parchment, to a baking sheet and prick it all over with a fork. Bake for 5 to 8 minutes, or until golden. Transfer to a wire rack and let cool. Repeat with the remaining dough disks.

Wrap the bottom of the springform pan tightly with aluminum foil. To assemble the cake, trim the first cake layer with kitchen scissors to fit in the pan, reserving the trimming scraps in a bowl. Place the trimmed cake layer in the pan and spread a layer of cream over it. Repeat the process with the remaining layers, covering the last layer with cream. Let the cake stand at room temperature for 6 hours, then refrigerate for 2 to 3 hours.

Blend or crush the reserved cake trimmings into fine crumbs. Carefully remove the sides from the springform pan, peel away the foil, and transfer the cake to a serving dish. Sprinkle the crumbs over the entire cake, covering it evenly. Toast the walnut halves in a frying pan over medium-high heat for 5 to 8 minutes, then roughly chop them. Sprinkle the nuts on top of the cake for decoration. Refrigerate again for at least 1 hour or up to overnight for the best flavor and texture.

NOTE

Just like French cuisine, Odesan cooking thrives on small details. These nuances transform a dish, making it truly unique. Lemon zest in the cream is quite unusual for Napoleon cake. I usually add the zest of 4 lemons to the cream along with vanilla, which makes it even more delicious. That's why, at every family celebration, my Napoleon cake was always the perfect grand finale to a rich, festive meal.

Maman's Honey Cake

Maman's Honey Cake

Tata founded a small group of wildly popular restaurants called Maman that serve authentic Odesan cuisine in an elevated style. Patisserie is one of the main attractions there. This honey cake is an iconic Ukrainian recipe, and Maman's version, which uses three types of cream instead of the usual one, constantly runs out. Maman's Honey Cake is both delectable and stunning to look at, as everything that Tata touches turns into beauty, just like her.

CREAM "IRISKA"

14 oz (400 g) condensed milk (in an unopened can)

DOUGH

2 eggs

7 oz (200 g) superfine (caster) sugar

3½ oz (100 g) honey

2½ teaspoons (15 g) baking soda

3½ oz (100 g) unsalted butter

15 oz (425 g) all-purpose flour, plus more for dusting

To prepare the cream "iriska," place the unopened can of condensed milk in a large pot. Fill the pot with enough water to completely cover the can by at least ¾ inch (2 cm). Bring to a boil then reduce to a simmer and cook for 3 hours, adding more water if the level gets too low. Let the can cool to room temperature, then open the can, transfer the caramelized cream to a bowl, and let cool completely.

To prepare the dough, in a large bowl, lightly whisk together the eggs, superfine sugar, honey, and baking soda. Place the bowl over a small saucepan of boiling water, making sure the bowl doesn't touch the water, and adjust the heat to low. Add the butter and let the mixture melt over the steam, stirring constantly, until the sugar is completely dissolved. The mixture should be homogeneous, smooth, and airy; it should turn pale brown in color and double in size. Remove the bowl from the heat and sift in the flour. Stir with a wooden spoon until the dough comes together evenly. Let the dough stand for a few minutes until warm to the touch but not hot. Sprinkle a work surface with a little flour. Transfer the dough to the work surface, shape into a ball, cover with a kitchen towel, and let cool.

Preheat the oven to 350°F (180°C).

Divide the dough into 8 equal pieces. On a sheet of parchment paper, roll out each piece into a circle about ⅛ inch (3 mm) thick. Use a plate with a diameter of 9½ inches (24 cm) to cut out a perfect circle from each one, reserving any dough scraps. Transfer each layer, still on the parchment, to a baking sheet. Bake each layer for 5 to 8 minutes, or until golden brown. (You can bake 2 layers at a time.) Let them cool completely, still on the parchment, on a wire rack. Bake the leftover dough scraps too; you will later crush those into crumbs to decorate the finished cake.

CUSTARD

7 oz (200 g)
superfine (caster) sugar

3 eggs

1 oz (25 g) all-purpose flour

About 2¼ cups (17 fl oz/500 ml)
cold whole milk, divided

7 oz (200 g) cold unsalted butter

SOUR CREAM FILLING

18 oz (500 g) sour cream
(at least 30% fat)

7 oz (200 g) confectioners' sugar

SERVES 10

To prepare the custard, in a small bowl, mix the superfine sugar, eggs, and flour. Add about ¾ cup (7 fl oz/200 ml) of the milk, mixing well with a whisk. Strain the mixture through a fine-mesh sieve so there are no lumps. Pour the remaining milk into a saucepan, set over low heat, and bring to a boil, stirring constantly. Slowly pour in the egg mixture, stirring vigorously. Cook, stirring constantly so the mixture doesn't stick, until it thickens. Cut the cold butter into cubes and add to the hot custard, then remove from the heat. Stir until the butter is completely combined. Transfer the custard to a bowl, cover with plastic wrap, and refrigerate until completely cool.

To prepare the sour cream filling, in a bowl, using a spoon or spatula, mix the sour cream and confectioners' sugar until smooth. Do not whisk.

To assemble the cake, place the first cake layer on a serving plate and spread one-quarter of the custard over it. Place the second layer on top and spread with another layer of custard. Spread half of the sour cream on the third layer; "iriska" cream on the fourth layer; another one-quarter of the custard on the fifth layer; the remaining sour cream on the sixth layer; "iriska" cream on the seventh layer; and the remaining custard on the eighth and final layer. Place the baked dough scraps in a blender and process until fine crumbs form. Pat the crumbs around the top and sides of the cake, covering all the cream.

Cover the cake with plastic wrap and refrigerate for at least 6 hours or up to overnight to allow the layers to soften and the flavors to meld.

NOTE

In Odesa you can buy caramelized condensed milk. If you can find something similar where you live, this will save you some time. You can also prepare this in advance as the ready-made condensed milk can be stored for a long time in an unopened can.

COFFEE & MACARONS

Easter Bread "Paska"

Easter Bread "Paska"

Marina is a cake maker known for her quirky, highly original creations, which are as bold and as rock 'n' roll as Marina herself. However, this recipe is very traditional, passed on to her by her grandmother Yuliya, who taught her that you need to "talk to" the rich, buttery dough while you knead it to wish health and prosperity to all those who end up eating the bread. Marina's grandmother is now in her eighties but the moment she touches the dough, it's as if the energy of her thirty-year-old self takes over. Yuliya lights up and sparkles, and when she talks about the process of baking and cooking, it's as if she describes magic. No wonder her granddaughter Marina sells out of her paskas the moment she puts the word out!

A pinch of saffron

1 teaspoon warm water

10½ oz (300 g) raisins (a mix of golden and dark)

All-purpose flour for sprinkling

STARTER

About 2¼ cups (17 fl oz/500 ml) whole milk

3½ oz (100 g) fresh yeast

1 tablespoon granulated sugar

1 tablespoon all-purpose flour

DOUGH

14 oz (400 g) unsalted butter, at room temperature, plus more for greasing

10 egg yolks

14 oz (400 g) granulated sugar

Seeds from 1 vanilla bean or 1 teaspoon vanilla paste

Zest of 1 lemon

½ teaspoon ground cardamom

Semolina flour for sprinkling

In a small bowl, soak the saffron in the warm water, then let it bloom. In another small bowl, sprinkle the raisins evenly with some flour.

To prepare the starter, warm the milk a little, no higher than 113°F (45°C). In a medium bowl, dissolve the yeast in the milk, add the granulated sugar and flour, and stir. Leave the mixture in a warm place to proof for about 30 minutes; it should be growing and increasing in volume. If it is not growing and increasing in volume, you will need to make a new dough starter.

To prepare the dough, melt the butter and let cool slightly. In a large bowl, beat the egg yolks with the granulated sugar until pale and fluffy. Pour in the warm butter (the butter should not be too hot or it will cook the eggs) and mix well. Add the vanilla, the saffron with the soaking water, the lemon zest, and cardamom. Add the dough starter and mix.

Sift the 2 pounds flour and add to the egg-butter mixture. Start kneading the dough, adding the raisins midway through the process. It's much easier to use an electric mixer fitted with the dough hook attachment, as kneading the dough by hand will take at least an hour or more. Don't be tempted to add more flour. Place the dough in an oiled bowl, cover with plastic wrap, and leave in a warm place. Proofing may take 3 to 7 hours because the dough is so buttery and will rise slowly. You want it to increase in volume by about one-third; you will begin to see the plastic wrap swelling slightly.

Butter 10 to 12 baking tins (any size of round molds work well) and sprinkle with the semolina flour. When the dough has increased by one-third, knead it again briefly and divide it among the prepared tins, filling each about two-thirds full. Leave the dough again in a warm place to proof until it increases by another one-third, about 1 hour.

Preheat the oven to 350°F (180°C).

ICING

1 lb (450 g) confectioners' sugar

2 egg whites

Juice of ¼ lemon

MAKES 10–12

Bake the paskas for 40 to 50 minutes. While they're still hot, carefully remove them from the baking tins, place on a wire rack, and let cool completely.

To prepare the icing, pour the confectioners' sugar into a high-sided bowl and add the egg whites and lemon juice. Using an electric hand mixer fitted with the whisk attachment, beat on high speed until the icing is thick enough to hold its shape.

When the paskas are completely cool, top them with the icing. The paskas will stay fresh for a very long time. They are at their best on the second day after baking.

NOTE

The baking time, color, and even taste of paska depend on the dish you use. The easiest option is to bake it in small panettone molds, which are made from self-supporting aper. You can also use round, deep ceramic or nonstick tins.

Small Rolled Cookies "Rohalyky" Stuffed with Plum Jam and Walnuts

Small Rolled Cookies "Rohalyky" Stuffed with Plum Jam and Walnuts

I am so grateful to Victoria for sharing the story and the recipe of her Jewish grandma Malka-Sulva Friedman. When Malka was young, she had to change her name to Maria, as did many people with Jewish, Greek, and Italian backgrounds during Soviet times. The dough for these cookies is rolled incredibly thin but is super easy to make. There are many alternatives to the filling offered here: You can use any jam and add with nuts or cookie crumbs, or finely chopped walnuts with sugar and ground cardamom, or raisins with nuts and candied orange peel. The main thing is to combine something sweet and soft with something a little crunchy, plus a contrasting flavor. But the most unexpected ingredient in Odesan *rohalyky* cookies is . . . beer! You don't need to worry about the aftertaste, though. The alcohol will evaporate during baking, creating pockets of air that make the cookies tender and crisp.

9 oz (250 g) unsalted butter

18 oz (500 g) all-purpose flour, plus more as needed

Sea salt

About 1 cup (9 fl oz) (250 ml) beer

3½ oz (100 g) walnuts

12¼ oz (350 g) plum or apple jam

Confectioners' sugar for dusting

MAKES 64

Melt the butter in a small saucepan over low heat, taking care to not let it boil. Let cool slightly. Sift the flour into a small bowl and mix in a pinch of salt. In a large bowl, combine the beer and melted butter, then gradually add the flour. You may need an additional 1½ oz (50 g) of flour if the dough is still sticky after kneading. The dough should be soft and not sticky, but be careful not to overwork it. Once kneaded, shape the dough into a ball, place it in a bowl, and cover with plastic wrap. Refrigerate for 30 to 50 minutes.

Meanwhile, toast the walnuts in a frying pan over medium-high heat. Let cool, then chop the walnuts into quarters.

Preheat the oven to 350°F (180°C).

Remove the dough from the fridge and divide it into 8 balls, about 4¼ oz (120 g) each. Work with one ball at a time and keep the remaining balls in the fridge, covered with plastic wrap.

Roll out the dough ball on a lightly floured work surface until about ¹⁄₁₆ inch (2 mm) thick and cut it into 8 equal triangles. For each cookie, place ½ teaspoon of the jam and a walnut piece on the wider end of each triangle, then roll into a crescent shape. Arrange about 32 cookies on a baking sheet, leaving a little space between them.

Bake for 30 minutes, or until golden brown. Transfer the baking sheet to a wire rack and let cool for a few minutes, then transfer the cookies to the rack and cool completely. Repeat with the remaining dough. Generously dust the cookies with confectioners' sugar before serving.

Dumplings with Sour Cherries

Privoz is an old market in the center of Odesa that is the beating heart of the city. When I was small, I would often visit the market with my mum. Traders would give me a piece of fruit or a pickled gherkin as a snack while my mother would drag me around the market to do her shopping. I loved it and so did Florina, who found me on Instagram because of my food posts. Florina was a child when her family left Odesa and moved to Israel, but she still remembers going to Privoz Market with her parents. When I invited her to take part in the book, she immediately agreed and chose her favorite *varenyky* (dumpling) recipe. Sour cherries are very hard to get in Israel, where we shot the photos for this recipe, but we managed to find some. You can swap in regular cherries; just halve the amount of sugar.

DOUGH

9¾ oz (280 g) all-purpose flour, plus more for dusting

Sea salt

2 tablespoons sunflower oil

¾ cup (6 fl oz/180 ml) whole milk

CHERRY FILLING

14 oz (400 g) fresh sour cherries

1 oz (30 g) superfine (caster) sugar

2 tablespoons (15 g) cornstarch

CHERRY SAUCE

1¾ oz (50 g) fresh sour cherries

1 oz (30 g) superfine (caster) sugar

1 cinnamon stick

1 whole clove

1 star anise

FOR SERVING

1¾ oz (50 g) unsalted butter

7 oz (200 g) sour cream

Confectioners' sugar for sprinkling

SERVES 4–6

To prepare the dough, in a large bowl, combine the flour, ½ teaspoon salt, and the sunflower oil. In a saucepan, bring the milk to a boil over medium-high heat. Add it to the bowl and mix with a wooden spoon to form a shaggy dough. Let the dough cool slightly, then knead it by hand or with an electric mixer until it comes together.

To prepare the filling, remove the pits from the 14 oz (400 g) cherries and place the cherries in a medium bowl. Add the superfine sugar and cornstarch and mix. Set aside.

To prepare the sauce, remove the pits from the 1¾ oz (50 g) cherries and place the cherries in a saucepan with about ½ cup (150 ml) water. Add the superfine sugar, cinnamon stick, clove, and star anise. Bring to a boil over high heat, then reduce the heat and simmer for about 10 minutes. Remove the whole spices and blend the cherry mixture with an immersion blender. Set aside for serving.

Roll out the dough to a thickness of about 1⁄16 inch (2 mm). Using a 2¾-inch (7-cm) pastry ring, cut out circles from the dough. Place 3 cherries in the center of each circle and fold over the dough to form a half-moon shape. Place on a well-floured work surface.

Fill a large saucepan with water, add a pinch of salt, and bring to a boil over high heat. Using a slotted spoon, gently drop the dumplings one by one into the boiling water, making sure none of them stick to the bottom of the pan. Boil for about 3 minutes, or until they float to the top.

Place the butter in a bowl. Using the slotted spoon, carefully transfer the dumplings to the bowl. Don't stir with a spoon; instead, shake the bowl so the dumplings can move around in the butter. Once all the dumplings are in the bowl and evenly coated with butter, add the cherry sauce and shake the bowl again. Transfer the dumplings to individual plates, add 1 tablespoon of the sour cream to each portion, and sprinkle confectioners' sugar on top.

NOTE

You can use frozen pitted cherries instead of fresh ones for this recipe. Defrost them slowly in the fridge and drain well before cooking. Reserve the drained juice for the sauce.

Dumplings with Sour Cherries

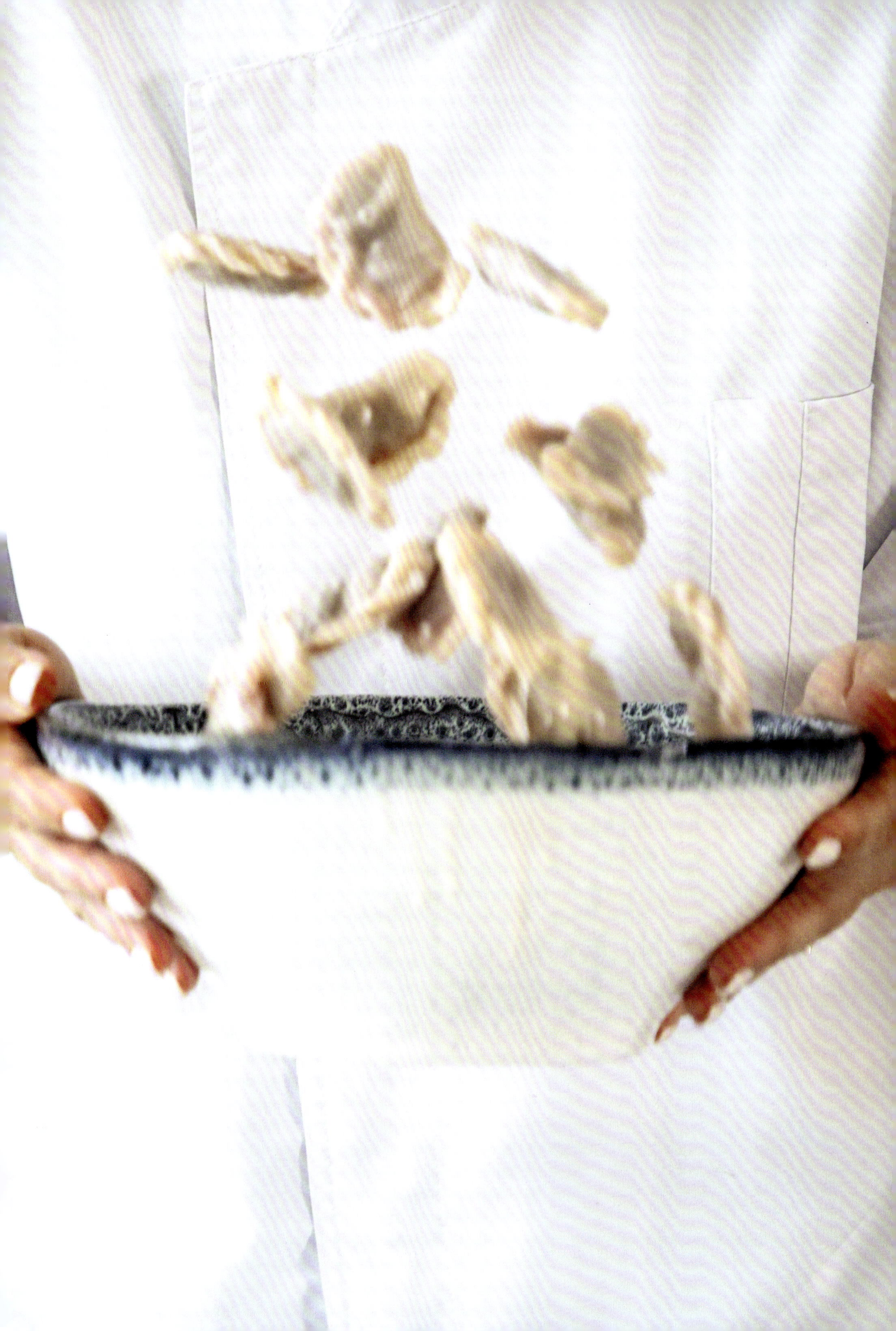

Odesan Terms and Traditions

MAMAN (AND THE ODESAN GRANNY)

Maman is a vivacious and voluptuous woman of a certain age who is the central force of Odesa's communities (see more on *dvoriks*, page 291). She is a superwoman who can seemingly do everything, with much panache and intelligence: hold down a full-on job (like a factory director or a housewife managing a busy household); be an exceptional cook (getting up at 5 a.m. to go to the market and stock up for a three-course dinner); and look great too (always with full makeup and accessories, even when going to the market or the beach).

Maman is usually in a solid marriage of many decades, or maybe freshly (re!)married to someone younger, or happily single. In every case, she is the boss. *Maman* is a matriarch in the oldest and truest sense. She looks after and protects (sometimes overprotects!) her family, neighbors, and everyone who comes in contact with her. *Maman* has opinions and is not afraid to share them. In fact, you'd be a fool not to listen because she has the wisdom of a wild woman or perhaps an old owl. When *Maman* becomes a grandmother, her sole purpose in life becomes feeding her grandchildren five or six meals a day. She initiates future Odesans into the importance of buying good food and eating well, teaching them how food is far more than just filling your belly.

PRIVOZ AND NEW MARKETS

All Odesans are divided into those who are devoted either to the Privoz Market or to the New Market, the two most important markets in the city.

The New Market was founded in 1896 and now its elegant buildings have been granted the protected status of architectural monuments. The Black Odesa variety of wine was developed here at the first center for enology (winemaking) over a century ago. When I do my gastronomic tours in Odesa, I bring people to the New Market to buy all the ingredients we'll then use to make our dinner. This market is relatively small, cozy, and well-behaved. We can enjoy chatting with vendors and choosing the best produce at a leisurely pace. I love how this market is steeped in history but also gives people the sense of Odesa's modern-day vitality.

Privoz Market is loud, chaotic, and fun. We have a saying in Odesa that you can buy anything in the world at Privoz This is the oldest market in Odesa, situated very close to the main train station, so it's easy for vendors from Odesan and neighboring areas to come here. You can still buy produce directly from those who grow it, which is such a rare privilege these days. You can ask farmers for advice, walk around sampling ingredients before you buy anything, and haggle (please do!). We joke that students, who are always hard up, get their three meals a day here at the market (they do!). There's something of an Eastern or Arab feel to the market, with the gorgeous displays of produce and the banter and noise all around. In fact, we use the word "bazaar," originally a Persian word, for our markets. These days Privoz is a very efficient machine that has kept up with the times. You can order produce over the phone or have a contract with vendors to deliver stuff to you. Good vendors are treasured and passed on from one generation to another like valuable antiques. For this book we bought pretty much everything at Privoz

TO "MAKE A BAZAAR"

This phrase says so much about Odesa that I could write a thesis on it! But I'll try to summarize. Odesa is a city primarily based on trade, and markets are places where people come not only to buy produce but also to boast about their new clothes, exchange news, gossip, share recipes, catch up with friends, teach their children important life lessons (like how to buy good food and make connections), and so on. Here you can sample the flavors of all sorts of cultures and ethnicities. The markets are our true multicultural melting pots. Here are some rules of the bazaar: sample and touch everything before buying, choose the best-quality products, talk to vendors and other shoppers because the connections you make here will last you a lifetime, bring a few bags or a trolley or even a suitcase, dress well (heels and lots of makeup will come in handy) but be practical, come hungry but don't forget a shopping list. Enjoy it, you are making a bazaar, not just shopping!

KOMMUNALKA FLATS

Kommunalka, short for a communal flat, was a type of apartment where several families or individuals lived together, sharing a kitchen, bathroom, and toilet. *Kommunalkas* became very widespread during Soviet times when lots of people moved from villages to towns for work. But even before the Russian Revolution, in the nineteenth century, people from the same trade, like bakers, would rent one of these flats. *Kommunalkas* became cauldrons of creativity where, out of necessity, people from different ethnicities and backgrounds would have to cohabit: cooking, arguing, laughing, and learning from each other in the process. These flats became the laboratories for creating the Odesan cuisine that we now know. The residents couldn't *not* learn and borrow ideas from each other!

ODESAN *DVORIK* YARDS

If *kommunalka* flats are the cauldrons of creativity inside Odesa's apartment blocks, Odesan *dvoriks* are the same cauldrons outside. Old Odesan houses tend to be two or three stories high, with several buildings encircling a courtyard. Such architecture naturally created an enclosure, a cozy and protected space that would typically have benches, children's playgrounds, clotheslines, tables for picnics, and, of course, trees and plants. Residents would spend almost half the year outdoors in their *dvoriks* thanks to Odesa's mild weather, which lasts from April until almost November.

People would exchange recipes and dishes, observe and learn from each other, pass on tips, and create communal meals. The aromas and sounds of food being cooked, coming from the windows all around the *dvoriks*, is something you have to experience to appreciate. The mouthwatering smells would entice people to go up to a window and strike up a conversation, try the food, get some cooking tips. Even during Soviet days when many ingredients were scarce, people found ingenious ways to cook with very little and still get delicious results. To this day, happy occasions are celebrated together, and difficult situations are also shared.

It's not always easy to live in such a close-knit community (boundaries can be a bit blurred), but no one ever feels lonely, which I always think is the harshest of human conditions. Each Odesan *dvorik* has an arch to enter from the street. To me, these arches look like eyes that give you a glimpse into Odesa's soul.

DACHAS OR SUMMERHOUSES

The phenomenon of *dachas*, or summer cottages, is not unique to Ukraine, but here in Odesa we make a really big deal out of our *dachas*. During colder months, Odesans tend to live in the city apartments but starting from April or May, we move to our *dachas* en masse. *Dacha* buildings themselves are often very basic, rustic structures (although they can be luxury villas too), but this simplicity is part of their allure. We might only visit our *dachas* on weekends or move over whole households for six months; the *dacha* attraction is a pull of energy that no one can resist. There are rituals, decorating styles, and types of cooking associated with *dachas*. Certain dishes are all part of our *dasha* repertoire: grilled meat *shashliks*, pilafs, zucchini, freshly picked then fried, ripe tomatoes in a colorful salad, eggs shakshuka style, or a fish soup *ukha* cooked on fire. We wouldn't normally eat them in our city dwellings.

Because Odesa is a seaside city, we like to have our *dachas* close to the water. Spending time surrounded by nature is something Odesans have been doing since the city's inception. Originally the *dacha* district was the area called the French Boulevard, but as the city grew, more neighborhoods became *dacha* districts. Fontan district is one such area and most Odesan beaches are located there. In the past the Fontan district was where fountains were established for the periods of water-supply shortages (*fontan* means "a fountain"). These days the area feels like an elegant health resort with looked-after beaches and a well-organized Trasa Zdorovya, the path of health, an area with sports grounds, parks, spots for picnics, and relaxation. By the way, to say that something is not "*fontan*" is a common expression, meaning that something is not great, it's okay but really underperforming. A theater play can be not *fontan*, or a dish, or even a person's behavior.

ODESAN CATS

These felines are the real kings of the city. You'll always see gangs of stray cats in *dvorik* yards and along the seafront, running around or luxuriating in the sun. The cats are often regularly fed by a particular self-designated grandma. The proliferation of cats can be explained by Odesa's history as a wheat trading port that attracted mice, which in turn attracted cats. They are so beloved by Odesans that there is even a series of statues dedicated to them. One very famous statue was erected in the New Market as a tribute to Bazarina, a very fat cat who lived there and was loved (and fed!) by everyone.

WHITE ACACIA TREES

The white acacia with its opulent flowers is the symbol of the city. The trees were originally planted by the first mayor of Odesa, the French-born Richelieu, in the early nineteenth century, in a manner similar to Paris. Odesan citizens could get free seedlings to grow their own acacia trees. In the twentieth century a cake, chocolates, and even a long-running operetta were named White Acacia. If you find yourself in Odesa in late spring or early summer, you'll be intoxicated by the aroma of white acacia in bloom. Like brides in billowy white dresses, there's something joyful and regal about this sight. You'll feel lighter and happier without even knowing why!

NEW YEAR'S EVE CELEBRATION

Many Odesans would describe the New Year's celebration as the biggest and most exuberant holiday of the year. The significance of this celebration goes back to Soviet times when Christmas, like all religious festivities, wasn't allowed. December 31 became the day that combined the focus on family with having a jolly good time with your friends and neighbors. People of all denominations, backgrounds, and religions come together around a table, forgetting any differences and woes of the previous year. The Odesan region is the most multicultural in Ukraine, so having a celebration like this is really important. We have no specific dishes or rituals for the New Year's table, except for one—at midnight we open a bottle of Ukrainian sparkling wine (the most popular one is called, surprise, surprise, "Odesa") and wish everyone a happy New Year. At least for a few moments, we all truly believe in magic.

FEASTS OF ODESA

I first learned about the existence of UNESCO's list of Intangible Cultural Heritage of Humanity when French gastronomic feasting was added to it in 2010. I was amazed that something so seemingly ephemeral was included but understood straightaway why. Such rituals can and do disappear, like many physical monuments, and they require protection. I believe the Odesan feast is also unique and in need of protection. In fact, the name of this book and the whole idea came from my desire to keep this heritage alive. When you read the stories I have included, I hope, and I know, you'll agree with me.

An Odesan feast includes a sense of ceremony and tradition. The meal starts with a trip to the market to buy the ingredients and, just as importantly, to "make a bazaar" (see page 290). The seasons, the occasion for celebration, and everyone's tastes determine the menu and the dishes to be made. Once back home the preparation is done, often together with family, friends, or neighbors. Parents pass on gestures and knowledge to the children. Neighbors and friends share tips and the all-important "nuances." Throughout the process, people exchange knowledge, advice, skills, and recommendations.

Then the meal proper begins with *zakuski* (appetizers) and ends with dessert, with several courses in between. Philosophy, exchange of local news, big and small ideas, and, especially, humor are all part of the flow of conversation. The feast involves all the senses: the aromas, the sight of how the table is set, the sounds of clinking utensils, the conversation and sounds coming from the *dvorik* courtyard outside. Any Odesan who moves away from their hometown will always love and miss their city: the sea, the architecture, the people, but most especially the food and our feasts.

Acknowledgments
дякую (Thank you)

This book is something I've been dreaming of for years. When I first embarked on the project, I had no idea how much time and work are involved in producing a cookbook. There are so many amazing people who have helped, encouraged, and contributed along the way. This single page at the back doesn't seem enough to do everyone justice, but here goes . . .

Arthur Geuchmann—for that moment when you exclaimed, "You must write a cookbook about Odesan food!"

To my dear publishers at Weldon Owen, it's a huge team, and there are many to thank. But especially Roger and Amy—your gentle handholding, patience, and encouragement have been so nurturing, pushing me forward and spurring me on. I knew I was in the right place from our very first meeting, and together, we realized and captured the essence of this book. You built the perfect team around me, you believed in me, and you showed so much kindness and patience all the way through the process. Thank you for allowing me this opportunity and supporting me as you have.

To my dear Andrew Nurnberg Associates team—Sarah, Lucy, and Michael—who have been there from the very start. You saw something in me when I was just a Ukrainian dreamer obsessed with Odesan food, and you helped me to realize my dream. Thank you for all the guidance, advice, and support over the years—what a journey it's been!

Barry Cunningham—for your attention and your visits to Odesa and our magical meeting at London's Savile Club in 2022, which was the start of a story that unfolded in the most enchanting way. Magic!

To all my photographers, both in Odesa and elsewhere—Elena Groza, Aleksandra Belinskaya, Anya Gusakova, Yuliia Pashentseva, Lisa Sheremet, Natali Levshina, Anat Peiser, Juliette Turrini, Andrew Rafael, Dmitry Skvortsov, Alexandr Synelnikov, Angelina Golt, Vika Geyder, Sabina Almasova, Julia Loza, Rumen Sarandev, Daria Kostenko, Anastasia Melnik—what a pleasure you are to work with. Your special talents have made this book so beautiful!

Ukrainian artists Irina Goncharenko and Olga Tokarenko—for the stunning and inspiring pictures.

Tolik Svinina, Olga, Modestovich, Vikusya, and all the vendors at Privoz Market—for making it possible, even in difficult times, to find the very best ingredients, including deep-sea turbot, the queen of the Black Sea.

Anastasia Malyarchuk and her mother, Alla—for instilling in me a love for good food and beauty since I was a child, for your friendship, for our childhood recipe, and for believing in me and my ideas!

Felicity Spector—for your brilliant networking, which made this book a reality, for your help with the photo shoots and recipe translations, and for being just as excited about this book as I am. And of course, for making the foreword full of tears and laughter.

Natasha MacAller, the Dancing Chef—for pushing me to take the first steps, for erasing all of my many doubts with kind words, a beautiful smile, and a sparkle in your eyes, even though we were thousands of miles apart.

Sergey and Elena Ivanova—you carried me through this entire journey, creating a solid foundation in the toughest situations. A special thank-you for your lessons in love and kindness.

Elena Vorozheikina—for your endless help along the way with everything in life, and for your incredible friendship.

Oleksandr Baron—for the steady shoulder I could always lean on and for your beautiful photographs.

Valentina Petrushenko—you are the best culinary assistant and food photographer in the world—and you are also the best foodie partner in crime.

Olya Zharova—for your strong desire to help me bring this book to life, a dream that took a decade to become a reality.

Lina and Fadey Perlov—for teaching me a concept that you called "interesting difficulties." It helped the book come to life and was a crucial part of this journey.

Infinite gratitude for Katerina Kollegaeva. Thank you for putting your heart and soul into the English translation. Talking about Odesa in English, translating all my Odesan idioms—that wasn't easy, but you managed it!

Elena Platonova—for your incredible diligence and capacity for hard work under any conditions.

This book never would have happened without my London friends Natalia Markland and Marianna Moldavskaya. Thanks for always believing that I would make it.

Charles Martell—for the lesson on the importance of having a mission in life.

James Felton Somers Hervey-Bathurst—for the incredible experience of our cooking school in Eastnor Castle, for your moral support during the war, and for waiting for this book to be born.

To Olya Graf—for Bake for Ukraine and your big heart, which warms so many people.

Yevhenii Holubovskyi—for teaching me to love my hometown and to see how the city responds in kind, guiding and supporting you even in the most difficult moments. You will live in my head and in my heart forever.

Elena Yakubsfeld—for your love, challah, and bracha for the book's success.

Regina, Natasha, Eugene Demenok, and Lena Lebedinskaya—for your strong support and for giving me the feeling of the "Odesan mafia"—in the best sense of the word.

Julia Suchshenko, Oksana Kuznetsova, Katya Kurlap, and Valery Suntsov—for our shared and unwavering love for our beautiful city.

Limor Chen—for the unique recipe and the incredible family story that all began in Odesa.

Olia Hercules—for inspiring me to promote my country's culture through food.

Skye McAlpine—your books helped me overcome depression and find a new meaning in life—in writing a book about my beloved Odesa.

Max Lagunov and Elena Matveeva—for successfully launching the book in Odesa, which introduced it to so many fascinating people.

Angela Olenich, Elena Radchenko, Alyona Yaremenko, Inna Nikolaeva, and Eugen Lemberg—for your wonderful recipes and financial support, without which I wouldn't have been able to complete this book.

Olena Tatyanchenko—for my culinary blog, where it all began.

To the volunteer team of the Restoration Workshop "1000 Doors of Odesa" and "Architecture of Odesa"—for the photographs and the incredible work they do every day to preserve the city's heritage.

To the eternal city of Odesa and its people—for the inspiration, the recipes, and the desire to make their mark on the gastronomic map of the world.

To all my friends—I want to say thank you for your loyalty and friendship, despite my absence. Now that this project is finished, I vow to be more present.

Karina, Leshya, and their big Ukrainian family—for making it less terrifying to spend an entire year in a basement while this book was being produced, hiding from the bombings over my hometown.

To our Ukrainian soldiers—for making it possible to photograph the majority of this book in a free Ukrainian Odesa. Glory to Ukraine!

To Oleg, the best husband in the world—for enduring these ten long years, first my "pregnancy" when I came up with the idea, then the book's production, for diligently devouring the dishes from this book during all my recipe testing, and—let's be honest—for helping prepare many of them, too.

To my son, Felix—who, I'm sure, will become my most devoted reader and the main champion of these recipes from his hometown. Everything I do is for you and your future children.

I dedicate this book to my parents, grandparents, and ancestors—whose fates, professions, passions, choices, victories and defeats, happiness and sorrows became the foundation of this beautiful and intricate puzzle that I have finally pieced together.

Index

D

R

S

T

U

V

W

Y

Z

34

weldon**owen**
an imprint of Insight Editions
P.O. Box 3088
San Rafael, CA 94912
www.weldonowen.com

CEO Raoul Goff
SVP Group Publisher Jeff McLaughlin
VP Publisher Roger Shaw
Executive Editor Edward Ash-Milby
Assistant Editor Kayla Belser
Managing Editor Michelle Hope
VP Creative Chrissy Kwasnik
Art Director Megan Sinead Bingham
Production Design Jean Hwang
VP Manufacturing Alix Nicholaeff
Senior Production Manager Joshua Smith
Strategic Production Planner Lina s Palma-Temena

Photographers Valentina Petrushenko, Elena Groza, Aleksandra Belinskaya, Anya Gusakova, Yuliia Pashentseva, Lisa Sheremet, Natali Levshina, Anat Peiser, Juliette Turrini, Andrew Rafael, Dmitry Skvortsov, Alexandr Synelnikov, Angelina Golt, Vika Geyder, Sabina Almasova, Julia Loza, Rumen Sarandev, Daria Kostenko, and Anastasia Melnik.

Cover Illustration by Daryna Berezhna.
Cover Concept by Irina Goncharenko.

Weldon Owen would also like to thank Amy Marr.

ISBN: 979-8-88674-173-5

Manufactured in China by Insight Editions

10 9 8 7 6 5 4 3 2 1

Insight Editions, in association with Roots of Peace, will plant two trees for each tree used in the manufacturing of this book. Roots of Peace is an internationally renowned humanitarian organization dedicated to eradicating land mines worldwide and converting war-torn lands into productive farms and wildlife habitats. Roots of Peace will plant two million fruit and nut trees in Afghanistan and provide farmers there with the skills and support necessary for sustainable land use.